STRATEGIC PASTOR

Become the Pastor your Church Needs

Matt Pilot

I dedicate this book to my father, Larry Pilot. He has always been my pastor. Through his investment in my life, he has touched the lives of many people. This is the essence of what being a Strategic Pastor is all about – impact one who will impact others.

A Note From the Author

Throughout this book, I reference the pastor in the male gender and not in the female. The reason I do this is solely for the purpose of writing style. I wanted to keep the flow of my thoughts as clear and to the point as possible. But let me clear. I completely believe in women being leaders and pastors within the church. I have done much Biblical study on this subject, and have conferred with Bible teachers who agree with this understanding. I hope that both men and women who aspire to be a pastor, or who wish to improve in their craft as a pastor will read this book and gain insight to enhance their calling.

Table of Contents

Introduction

What do you think of when you think of a pastor? Do you have good feelings or bad?

It depends on your experience.

If you grew up in church, you have some understanding of a pastor, or Priest. You may have called the Priest "Father". If you grew up in the Southern part of America, you may have heard your dad call them "Preacher." You may have thought the pastor's first name was "Preacher" because your dad always addressed him as "Hey, Preacher! That was a good sermon today."

If you did not grow up in church, your idea of a pastor could be that of a quiet man living in solitude strolling around a dark, empty church all day long. You have seen the movies with a man dressed in a black suit with a tight, white collar around his neck, who was always available to anyone who cared to stop by the church or parish to answer spiritual questions.

If you are a follower of popular culture over the years, you have seen tele-evangelists with charismatic speeches preaching to a camera in an elaborate television studio, with pre-recorded audiences who applaud on cue. Or, you have seen a live-televised church service where the cameras pan people singing, crying or showing much emotion as the pastor shouts and screams.

My first picture of what a pastor looks like was observing my dad. My dad was the pastor of our church in Turlock, California back in the eighties and nineties. He not only pastored the church, he founded it. Before starting the church, my dad had been an Associate pastor, focusing on music and youth ministries. He and my mom felt God call them to start a church, with the support and urging of a few families and with the encouragement of another pastor nearby, who had become their mentor.

My earliest recollection of church was in an old American Legion Hall in the older part of a small town, where our people gathered on Sundays. I remember seeing people set up chairs and prepare the Hall for church service. My dad would push the piano and podium in place, while my mom was down stairs setting up the children's area before families arrived. Back in those days, we did not have video, lighting, or billboards. No tv cameras, no beautiful facilities with new carpet and matching seats. I remember having kids church in the basement of that old American Legion Hall. I loved kids church. What I loved was not the facility, or the program, but the leaders. They loved us kids and had energy and passion. I do not remember all of the lessons, but I do remember the kids and I remember the loving people who voluntarily took the leadership roles of teacher and facilitator.

I watched my mom and dad be pastors. They were always giving to others. They were always leading by example. Whenever my dad got up on a Sunday to talk about money, he would first put his own check in to the offering plate while he asked people to sacrifice so that they could build the church stronger. I saw my dad and mom take on so many roles in the church. They sang, they organized, they served, they loved, they visited, they taught. They were always initiating, always reaching, always stretching so that the church would grow strong. Many people came through that church and grew spiritually because of it. That church became a leader of churches in our small town of Turlock in those years, and my mom and dad led the people of the church to financially sacrifice so they could buy property right off of the highway. They worked 7 years to build a church building, and they paid for it as they built. My dad would work all day, and then go home to get work clothes on and meet people at the church to work on building the church. They did not hire a company to build the church – they built it with their own hands. Anyone who had building experience would be asked to come build the church building. My mom was a school teacher, a mother of 3, a pastor's wife, and even she also would go and help.

I remember at Christmas time, my dad thought strategically how he could reach people with the message of Jesus. With the church being located on the main highway, he decided to craft a large, lighted sign that said "Glory to God in the Highest." People who drove by at night would see and comment how they saw the sign of that "church on the highway." My dad was so proud of that beautiful sign. Many nights, our family would drive by the church and pull over to see the sign shining big and bright over the church. This church represented my parent's life-long work. It was a home to many who had no home. It was a place where people could come to experience God and grow in their life.

That church stands today, reaching people and serving in the community. I was raised there, and found my love for God and for people.

I remember the church services we had, both on Sundays and on Wednesday nights. My dad would call our people forward to the altar. We did not have a former altar, so we used the steps near the platform as a makeshift altar. The reason we would kneel was to physically demonstrate our surrender and worship to God. In the Bible, you will find many ways men and women would respond to God, by kneeling, raising hands, clapping, singing, and reading the Bible out loud together. It was in those Sunday night and Wednesday night church services at the conclusion of my dad's message that many of us would respond to his call to give ourselves completely to God's purposes for our lives. My grandmother played the organ at the end of the service while my dad would speak to us, and would even allow God to speak through Him to our hearts. We would not be rushed. We would linger. We would talk to God, sing to God – and we would be quiet so that God may speak to us.

My dad's father was also a pastor. He was not just a pastor of a church; he also was what they called a Presbyter, meaning an overseer of pastors and churches. In his retirement, my grandfather helped my dad by helping with the care and counseling of the people. My grandfather was so happy to see me go off to Bible College to study for being a pastor, just as he had, like my dad had. He died while I was in school, and never saw me actually become a pastor.

My father, who has now been retired along with my mother, moved to South Florida to support me and my family as we are pastors. Like his parents, my father focuses on supporting me. My mom and dad sit right behind me in church every Sunday. They love our people. They invite people. They give to people. My dad will regularly text me or call me to tell me what a great pastor I am. He will say "your speaking was so amazing today – there is no one like you, Matt." And I will say "but dad, I didn't even preach! All I did was the greeting." He will respond "well, your greeting touched the hearts of people – they love you." My mom and dad are still pastors to me today. They are still pastors to hundreds of people who reach out to them from around the Country.

You may have many views of what a pastor is. You may have had a good pastor, or Priest. You may have had an average pastor. You may have been exposed to even an abusive pastor, or a person who mishandled leadership. Most people do not fully understand what pastors do. I had one family member who was curious about what I do as a pastor. He asked "do you just pray and read the Bible all day?" I smiled and told him that I do those things, but there is more to being a pastor than just praying and reading God's Word.

I am writing this book for anyone who is curious about what a pastor does, I am writing this book for anyone who, like me heard the voice of God call you to be a leader in the church, to be a pastor.

I want to explain what a pastor is, what he does, and what he should be focused on. As you have read about my mom and dad, my grandparents, you can see from my perspective how impactful a pastor can be. You can see the heart, the passion, the vision, the sacrifice, the commitment, the leadership that it takes to be an effective pastor.

Were my parents and grandparents successful as pastors? I would say yes. You know why? Because their son (and grandson) followed in their footsteps and is a pastor. I became a pastor because I saw my parents live in such a way that inspired me. Their example thrust me in to growing and learning to become more like Jesus.

I have a cute memory of when I was about 6 or 7 years old at a family's house on a Sunday night pool party. Sunday nights were fun because after church, one or two families would host social gatherings. Our church loved to get together to have fun together. At that time, I was the kid of the group hanging with kids older than me. I loved being with the older kids and looked up to them. At that time, I had just started piano lessons at five years old. My dad was an accomplished piano player and would play in church. This was in the year 1980, shortly after the blockbuster movie "Saturday Night Fever" was hot in culture. I remember some of the older kids asking the question in our group "what do you want to be when you grow up." I had never really thought about that. I blurted out "I want to be a piano player, a pastor, and a disco teacher." The group erupted with laughter! One of the girls, Nancy replied "that will be quite a combination!"

Well, I never became a disco teacher. In fact, I can't dance to save my life. However, I did become a piano player. And I did become a pastor.

In my years of being a pastor, I have learned the heart and the skills of being a pastor. My heart is for you. As you seek to become a pastor, or as you are currently a pastor and want to grow in your ability, I want to help you.

I have many friends, both men and women who are doing the work of a pastor. What saddens me is to see them discouraged and overwhelmed. They have questioned whether they are having any impact, wondering if they should just try something else. It breaks my heart to see good people doing good work in the church, but struggle with the many problems and obstacles. Pastors can deal with depression, with self-esteem, and with spiritual attack from Satan.

I see many pastors just surviving as they lead in their churches. I want to help you THRIVE in your church, not just survive. I want to give you permission to think a certain way. I want to challenge you to focus your limited energy and your limited time in a more strategic way to have great impact.

My prayer is that you will embody the calling of Strategic Pastor and find great fulfillment and success!

Chapter 1

Defining the Pastor's Role

Ephesians 4:11-12 KJV
And he gave some, apostles; and some, prophets; and some, evangelists; and some, **pastors** and teachers; For the perfecting of the saints, for the work of the ministry, for the edifying of the body of Christ...

What does a pastor do? How do we define exactly what the job description is for a pastor?

We see in the instruction of the Apostle Paul that there are various ministry roles in the church, all with the same purpose of preparing the saints to do ministry so that followers of Jesus can grow. Another translation says:

Ephesians 4:12 NLT
Their responsibility is to equip God's people to do his work and build up the church, the body of Christ.

I love those words EQUIP and BUILD UP. They are action-oriented words. They do not describe someone who is docile or hesitant. They describe intention and design. EQUIP and BUILD UP give clear definition to the purpose of a pastor. They are marching orders that require goal setting, strategy...and good, ole work ethic. Equipping and building takes hard work.

It's been said by veteran pastors many times:

"do you know how you spell revival? W.O.R.K."

It takes hard work to be an effective pastor. Anyone who has been a pastor for more than 30 days will tell you that being a pastor is demanding and intense. If you are called to be a pastor, it is wonderful. But you need to know it is not for the faint of heart.

I don't think most people realize how hard the work is. People see the pastor smiling and talking with someone at church. They see them leading in prayer. They see them serving with the team and think "wow, it must be nice to be paid to do what we all do voluntarily."

I remember watching my dad preach powerful sermons on Sundays as a young boy and thinking that it looked so fun and exciting. I loved that he would be dressed in a beautiful suit, would seem like he was having such a great time getting people to laugh, getting them to cry, getting them to respond to the message of Jesus. He would lead the church in song, in prayer, and in the vision of the church. I remember thinking that I wanted to do that.

It wasn't until I first became a pastor right out of Bible College that I realized the glitz and glamour of the Sunday platform was about 5% of it! All of the work and preparation took so much time and energy. By the time I got to Sunday, where all of the "fun stuff' happened, I was worn out! It took me all day Monday to resuscitate, so I could start again Tuesday. And that was in my twenties!

A few years ago, I had one man in my church who was successful in business. He came to our church and we became friends. However, he had his own opinions how he felt church should be. He told me he always felt God called him to be a pastor to have his own church. The man was bold and outspoken. He approached life with reckless abandon and did what he wanted to. I loved him and tried to give him guidance in his life when he would share his struggles, but he was resistant to any ideas but his own. He did more talking than listening. Consequently, areas in his life were not healthy and it affected his family and his relationships in the church. Being loose with his words and free with his attitude, I remember him one day telling me "I could pastor a church. It's easy!"

This man eventually left our church and went searching for another. He landed in a smaller church, likely because he thought that the smaller the church, the more he could get close to the pastor and have more control in how the church operated. Months later, I heard he left that church frustrated. I saw on Facebook that he and his wife had started their own church. But, lo and behold, it wasn't a few months later, and the church was off Facebook. He never really got the church established. What a sad story. It would have been so much better for this man to first be a pastor at home, and to come under the leadership of his pastor, staying committed and planted in the same church. Psalm 92:13 Those that are planted in the house of the Lord shall flourish in the courts of our God. NKJV

Not everybody should strive to be a pastor.
It looks exciting...and it is.

It looks easy... it is not.

When I meet aspiring leaders who share their dreams with me of being a pastor, I affirm them. I want to "stir up the gifts in them..." I Timothy 1:6. But, I also caution them about the cost of the calling. I tell them that most people should never work at the church, and most are not called to be a pastor of the church. Most people should make their living outside the church, so they can serve in their church. However, there are some that God places His hand on to step up and lead as pastor. The life of a pastor is a great life. But it is not for everybody:

It is a life of calling and commitment

It is a life of sacrifice and holy purpose

It is a life of giving of yourself and of giving yourself up

It calls for vision, energy, growth, and maturity

It demands passion and requires compassion

A great job description of what a pastor should be is found in the "Love Chapter":

Corinthians 13:4-7
Love is patient and kind. Love is not jealous or boastful or proud or rude. It does not demand its own way. It is not irritable, and it keeps no record of being wronged. It does not rejoice about injustice but rejoices whenever the truth wins out. Love never gives up, never loses faith, is always hopeful, and endures through every circumstance.

I call this famous scripture the "Love Chapter" because I am asked to read it at every wedding ceremony I lead. While this Bible passage is appropriate to describe the love of a man and woman uniting in marriage, it is really a picture of how Christ loves the Church. It is also a great picture showing how a leader leads and loves the people he is called to look after. If Christ loves the Church this way, the pastor should love the Church this way.

Pastors in the Bible

There are some great examples of people who led spiritually in the Bible. We see pictures of what a good pastor does. He cares for the people he is responsible to lead and guide.

Moses

Moses was a great leader of the Hebrews. He delivered them from their slavery in Egypt and led them in the wilderness, teaching them to become the Holy Nation of Israel. God used Moses to show these former slaves to know God and to properly live in relationship with Him.

It is interesting to me how God prepared Moses to become this famed leader in the Bible. I love to study the process of learning, and I am intrigued with people's story and struggle of becoming what they are destined to become. Moses learned his skills of pastoring people by looking after sheep in a remote mountain for forty years. Before that, he grew up in the royal palace of Egypt as a Prince. He FIRST learned how NOT to lead. He THEN learned HOW to lead.

The first experience in the palace taught him to lead by his position. He led by entitlement. Moses led people through fear, through exerting power. When you have a whip in one hand, and hold food in the other, you can intimidate and manipulate people to do what you want them to.

The later experience of herding sheep taught him you cannot force sheep to follow you; you must develop the art of leading them. You learn how to use your voice, your presence, and your shepherd's staff to herd the sheep. You are always looking to protect them from threat of danger. The role of a shepherd is not a high position. It is a role of tending to your flock. It has much responsibility with little entitlement.

The Bible also shows the character trait of Moses:

Numbers 12:3 NIV
Moses was a very humble man, more humble than anyone else on the face of the earth.

The years hidden in obscurity herding sheep had likely worn him down. It is said that humility is not thinking less of yourself, it is just thinking of yourself less.

Moses was always thinking what was best for the people he cared for.

What do *they* need?
What should *they* hear?
What should *they* do?
What should *they* stay away from?

Another role that Moses took was to help his people with difficult decisions, guiding them with wisdom in their day to day lives:

Exodus 18:13 NIV
...Moses took his seat to serve as judge for the people, and they stood around him from morning till evening.

The Bible gives us wonderful teaching and clear Theology to align our lives to. However, *the role of a pastor is to bring* **wise counsel** *and* **guidance** *to the people he looks after, helping them* **navigate** *through choices and difficult issues.*

Samuel

Samuel was born for leadership. At an early age, his parents brought him to the Priest placing him in his care and tutelage, living at the Priest's home. We see early on in Samuel's life his calling was to **hear God's voice** and to **speak it out**:

I Samuel 3:1-5 NIV
The boy Samuel ministered before the Lord under Eli. In those days the word of the Lord was rare; there were not many visions. One night Eli, whose eyes were becoming so weak that he could barely see, was lying down in his usual place. The lamp of God had not yet gone out, and Samuel was lying down in the house of the Lord, where the ark of God was. Then the Lord called Samuel. Samuel answered, "Here I am." And he ran to Eli and said, "Here I am; you called me."
Samuel played the role of Prophet and Judge over Israel. Before the era of Kings ruling in Israel, God raised up leaders, called Judges to guide the people. The word "Judge" means Judicial, meaning decisive, discerning the right course of action.

Samuel was one of the greatest leaders of Israel, and helped to transition the Nation of Israel from the times of Moses and Joshua to the era of King David, which would lead to the eventual building of the Temple of God in God's City, Jerusalem.

Samuel also embodied the office of Priest, standing in proxy for the Nation of Israel to ask for God's help in difficult circumstances:

1 Samuel 7:9-13
So Samuel took a nursing lamb and offered it as a whole burnt offering to the Lord. And Samuel cried out to the Lord for Israel, and the Lord answered him. As Samuel was offering up the burnt offering, the Philistines drew near to attack Israel. But the Lord thundered with a mighty sound that day against the Philistines and threw them into confusion, and they were defeated before Israel. And the men of Israel went out from Mizpah and pursued the Philistines and struck them, as far as below Beth-car.

Then Samuel took a stone and set it up between Mizpah and Shen and called its name Ebenezer; for he said, "Till now the Lord has helped us." So the Philistines were subdued and did not again enter the territory of Israel. And the hand of the Lord was against the Philistines all the days of Samuel.

In these ancient times, before Jesus and before the Holy Spirit in-dwelled in every Christian, people had to rely on the spiritual leader to communicate with God. Even now in our time, Christians still look to spiritual leaders who are more in tune with the heart of God and the voice of God for spiritual guidance. A pastor like Samuel can help clarify and affirm what God is wanting to say to the Christian.

Samuel was consecrated to the Lord, set apart for His holy purposes to spiritually lead the people in his care. A pastor in the same way is *set apart to spiritually lead and guide the people in his care*. Because of this, the pastor always remembers that what he is called to is a **sacred trust**, being **mediator** between God and man.

David

David is known as the greatest King of Israel. He is the King that successfully established the city of Jerusalem as the capital city of Israel. He conquered many enemies, and widened the borders of Israel. He captured back from his enemies the Ark of the Covenant, the symbol of God's power and presence.

Like Moses, David came from humble beginnings, starting as a shepherd. David came from the house of Jesse, and was the youngest and most forgotten of all of his father's sons. Yet, God saw the right qualities of leadership in David:

1 Samuel 16
But the Lord said to Samuel, "Do not consider his appearance nor his height, for I have rejected him. The Lord does not look at the things people look at. People look at the outward appearance, but the Lord looks at the heart.

So Samuel took the horn of oil and anointed (David) in the presence of his brothers, and from that day on the Spirit of the Lord came powerfully upon David.

David was a passionate man. He had unique skills he utilized to rule as King. He was a gifted songwriter and musician. He was also a gifted warrior and military general. These are two skills that you wouldn't think could co-exist in one person. David was a Warrior-Poet.

Because David was passionate, sensitive and courageous, he attracted great people to follow him. David learned the art of building influence and attracting people to him in his years running away from King Saul, who was jealous of him and wished to take his life:

1 Samuel 22:2
All those who were in distress or in debt or discontented gathered around him, and he became their commander. About four hundred men were with him.

Later, when David was King of Israel, we see great men of valor follow him, as described in 2 Samuel 23.

David had learned the art of leadership, observing both Samuel and also King Saul. He saw what worked, and what did not work. Coupled with his passion for God and compassion for people, this made David an effective leader.

The biggest reason David succeeded to lead for many years was that he did not just see himself as a positional leader as King or Commander. He always kept the mindset of shepherd:

Psalm 78:72
And David shepherded them with integrity of heart; with skillful hands he led them.

I love how this verse does not describe David ruling over them. It says "David shepherded them." The writer actually makes the noun "shepherd" a verb, to describe the position, not as ruler, but as caregiver and guide.
This verse is a beautiful equation of what a pastor does. It has two sides that balance one another:

Heart - Skill

David had a heart for God and for God's people with a pure motive.

David led with great skill and wisdom.

A pastor balances both sides of this delicate equation, **leading with integrity,** and **leading using skill.** *A pastor leads from his strengths and God-given skills.* David led with his sensitivity, his songwriting, and his military knowledge. A pastor draws from his unique personality and utilizes his gift set to **shepherd his people effectively.**

Jesus

Jesus is the perfect example for every leader and for every person. He is the ultimate standard we strive to reach for.

Jesus was born in the same region of Israel as King David, the region of Bethlehem. Jesus grew up in a humble setting, in a Carpenter's home.

I have always wondered if Jesus ever felt like He was misplaced, like God had assigned Him to the wrong family. Though his father Joseph loved His son, all he could do was teach Jesus what he knew: carpentry. While most boys enjoy working with tools and building things, it seems to me that Jesus may not have been interested in his father's career. We know in scripture when Mary and Joseph lost track of Jesus while on a family trip to Jerusalem. They found Jesus in the most unexpected place:

Luke 2:41-50 NIV
Every year Jesus' parents went to Jerusalem for the Festival of the Passover. When he was twelve years old, they went up to the festival, according to the custom. After the festival was over, while his parents were returning home, the boy Jesus stayed behind in Jerusalem, but they were unaware of it. Thinking he was in their company, they traveled on for a day. Then they began looking for him among their relatives and friends. When they did not find him, they went back to Jerusalem to look for him. After three days they found him in the temple courts, sitting among the teachers, listening to them and asking them questions. Everyone who heard him was amazed at his understanding and his answers. When his parents saw him, they were astonished. His mother said to him, "Son, why have you treated us like this? Your father and I have been anxiously searching for you."
 "Why were you searching for me?" he asked. "Didn't you know I had to be in my Father's house?"[a] But they did not understand what he was saying to them.

Jesus obeyed His parents, but he did not fit their mold. He was built differently. He was not interested in studying carpentry.

He was interested in studying the Holy Scriptures. He was fascinated with the deep, spiritual meanings of the scriptures.

We find Jesus later as an adult back in the Synagogue reading the scriptures:

Luke 4:16-20
He went to Nazareth, where he had been brought up, and on the Sabbath day he went into the synagogue, as was his custom. He stood up to read, and the scroll of the prophet Isaiah was handed to him. Unrolling it, he found the place where it is written:
"The Spirit of the Lord is on me,
    because he has anointed me
    to proclaim good news to the poor.
He has sent me to proclaim freedom for the prisoners
  and recovery of sight for the blind,
to set the oppressed free,
to proclaim the year of the Lord's favor."[1]
Then he rolled up the scroll, gave it back to the attendant and sat down. The eyes of everyone in the synagogue were fastened on him. He began by saying to them, "Today this scripture is fulfilled in your hearing."

Later, we read where the followers of Jesus called him "Rabbi", which means Teacher in the Hebrew language. Hebrew tradition describes a phase that was common to Jewish men saying to one another:

...may you be covered in the dust of the Rabbi

The idea was that followers who wanted to become more like their Teacher would follow so close behind him that, as a result, they would literally be covered in their dust from the road. To learn from your teacher, you must be in close proximity to them so you can pick up as much knowledge and wisdom as possible.

Jesus is described as many things. He is the perfect Leader. He is the Prophet, Priest, and King. He is the Lamb of God, the Anointed and promised Messiah. But, in our study of what a pastor is, I am drawing attention to Jesus as the great Rabbi, the great Teacher.

Albert Einstein was quoted as saying "The definition of genius is taking the complex and making it simple." Skilled teachers take complex principles and break it down in a simple way so they can transfer knowledge to their students.

Jesus taught the scriptures with such wisdom and with such power that common people could grasp their meaning. People literally changed their lives because of what Jesus taught. The world was turned upside down because of Jesus' teachings.
Jesus condensed the entire Law and the Ten Commandments when challenged by the Religious Teachers:

Matthew 22:35-40
One of them, an expert in religious law, tried to trap him with this question: "Teacher, which is the most important commandment in the law of Moses?"
Jesus replied: "Love the Lord your God with all your heart and with all your soul and with all your mind. This is the first and greatest commandment. And the second is like it: Love your neighbor as yourself."

A pastor is a **teacher** of God's Word, *and takes great care to present it in a way that connects to people so they can apply it practically to their lives. Not only did Jesus teach God's Word,* **He LIVED God's Word**. *The Apostles carried on Jesus' teaching and built His Church long after Jesus left Earth. The Church lives on through followers of Jesus who teach God's Word like Jesus did. Jesus' life changed our lives forever.*

Paul

Paul is an interesting character. He is introduced to us under another name, Saul. Saul was a well-studied Jewish man who grew up learning Holy Scripture under the best religious teachers of his time. Saul was a focused and passionate man. He was opinionated and was ambitious in his pursuits. Because he had not yet come to terms with the truth of who Jesus of Nazareth was, Saul was on mission to put down the heretical believers of Jesus, by imprisoning and even killing them.

Yet, Jesus desired to use this angry, driven man, Saul. Jesus confronted Saul by revealing His divinity to him one day on a road to Damascus. It was there that Jesus changed his name from Saul to Paul, and gave Him a holy assignment, to preach His message to the world. After this amazing encounter, Paul now used his focus and ambition to share the gospel of Jesus Christ.

Paul not only preached the Gospel message, he also established churches. Paul realized that his mission was not just to preach, it was to plant.

1 Corinthians 3:6
I planted the seed in your hearts, and Apollos watered it, but it was God who made it grow.

How Paul was able to plant so many churches in his time was by developing Christ followers in to leaders. Paul was a developer of people, and intentionally spent time teaching and investing in those who showed potential for more.

Paul developed many people to do great works. Two men he raised up to become pastors of churches were Timothy and Titus. In fact, the letters he wrote to them are famously studied as the "pastoral epistles."

Paul was a pastor to the pastors, and was a pastor over the churches. Some would call Paul a Bishop, meaning overseer of churches. So, while each church had a pastor, Paul was an overseer of that group of people, teaching and caring through their pastor.

Paul did this through writing letters. If he were alive today, he likely would have been the pastor of a multi-site church, teaching through video. I am a Campus Pastor at Christ Fellowship, and our church has Senior Pastors, Todd and Julie Mullins. In many ways, they are like the regional pastors, while I am the pastor over our Stuart Campus located in Martin County.

Paul not only brought **spiritual development** to the churches, he brought **systemic development** for the churches. His letters give **practical instruction** on order within the church. He gives guidelines for how to live, and describes qualifications for different positions in the church and for use of various gifts in the church.

Some pastors have the calling to plant churches. Others have the calling to water and grow churches. And yet, other pastors have the capacity to give oversight to pastors and churches, bringing strategy and structure so the churches can sustain health and impact in their community. The important thing to do as a pastor is to discern where you can have the greatest impact. You can't do everything, so what should you give yourself to? God will place you in different roles in different seasons of your life as a pastor. The key is understanding that whatever role God gives you to play is important in building His Church. That verse I mentioned earlier goes on to say:

1 Corinthians 3;7-8
It's not important who does the planting, or who does the watering. What's important is that God makes the seed grow. The one who plants and the one who waters work together with the same purpose. And both will be rewarded for their own hard work.

I love this verse! What is important is to understand your true purpose in being a pastor. Your job is to fulfill whatever role God gives you in growing the seed that God has placed in people's lives. Whatever your gift, whatever your part, you will be rewarded by God!

Play Your Role

While it is inspiring to study the lives of many people in the Bible, like Moses, Samuel, David, Jesus, and Paul, it is relieving to see how each of them played a specific role that God called them to.

So many others in the Bible played key roles in helping God's people flourish. What made them great was not their gift or skill. It was their availability and their obedience. Every person that God worked through was available and was obedient when He called on them. Rahab, Deborah, Esther, and Mary were some of the great woman who God worked through mightily to accomplish His holy purpose. God is always looking for an individual that is available and willing to obey what He asks.

Being available to God cannot come with your conditions. You may be more passionate with one aspect of leadership than another. That is understandable. I realize that God gives you passion for certain gifts He has planted in you. You should focus on the gifts that you are passionate about. I totally agree. But there must be a fundamental understanding that you are completely available to God. This means that you may not always get to operate only in your gift. There may be times that you have do to work that you do not enjoy. The first step to being a pastor, a Spiritual Leader of God's people is this: "Here I am, Lord!"

Isaiah

The Prophet, Isaiah had this available spirit when we see him respond to God's call:

Isaiah 6:8-9 NIV
Then I heard the voice of the Lord saying: Whom shall I send? Who will go for us?
And I said, "Here am I. Send me."

As I read of Isaiah's calling, I notice this: God's *call* comes before God's *conditions*. It is only after Isaiah shows his availability to God, that God then begins to outline the difficult task that He is asking of Isaiah. God is looking for an all-in heart. He is looking for someone who is not concerned with the role description. He wants dedication. He wants trust from those He will use.

Are you all in? Are you ready and available for how God wants to use you? Or are you only available with conditions? The first step of leadership is not to lead. It is not to pursue an education in learning ministry. It is simply you saying to God "Here am I. Send me!" This may mean that you start with cleaning toilets. You may start serving God by serving on the church traffic team out in the parking lot. If you want God to use you

> God's *call* comes before God's *conditions*

as a pastor, respond to Him with an open heart. Tell Him today that you are available. Play whatever role God puts in front of you TODAY. Do not worry if you cannot see the path to pastor right away. Let God worry about opening up doors and leading the way for you. If you respond to God, He will respond to you!

Playing your role also demands your obedience. Do whatever is asked of you, whenever you are asked. I heard one mother ask her son to do a chore in the house. He said he would do it. A couple of hours later, when she checked to see if the chore was done, it was not. She came to her son who was in his room playing video games, and asked why the chore was not done. The son replied "I am going to get to it." The mother said that he had disobeyed her request. He disagreed with her. She said "not obeying immediately is disobedience."

Not obeying God when he asks you to do something is to disobey Him. Not to fully complete God's instructions is disobedience. Trying to figure out a better way to do what God asks is not to obey. It is to circumvent. Obedience is full completion of the task, done immediately. Like right now.

When God saw Isaiah's availability, "Here I am", and saw his willingness to obey, "send me", God then could trust Isaiah with the plan:

Isaiah 6:9-13 NIV
He said, "Go and tell this people:
"'Be ever hearing, but never understanding; be ever seeing, but never perceiving.'

Make the heart of this people calloused;
    make their ears dull
    and close their eyes.[a]
Otherwise they might see with their eyes,
    hear with their ears,
    understand with their hearts,
and turn and be healed."
Then I said, "For how long, Lord?"
And he answered:
"Until the cities lie ruined
    and without inhabitant,
until the houses are left deserted
    and the fields ruined and ravaged,
until the Lord has sent everyone far away
    and the land is utterly forsaken.
And though a tenth remains in the land,
    it will again be laid waste.
But as the terebinth and oak
    leave stumps when they are cut down,
    so the holy seed will be the stump in the land."

As you read this, you see that Isaiah's assignment was difficult. God was sending him to speak to people who would be closed to Isaiah's message. How frustrating. Yet, God revealed a surprise at the end. Isaiah would be the voice that would introduce the coming of Messiah, the Anointed One. Isaiah's voice would echo through the pages of history to display the prophetic power and mystery of God to all generations. God was going to use Isaiah in bigger ways than Isaiah could ever comprehend. This happened because of Isaiah's attitude of God and his response to God. May we as pastors always be in a posture of availability and obedience to whatever God asks whenever He asks it.

Conclusion

Studying the life of Moses, Samuel, David, Jesus and Paul gains us insight into what a pastor is and what a pastor does in the church. We see a theme of Shepherd, of Leader, of connecting people to God and to God's Word. We see a life of holiness and holy purpose. We also understand that whatever role God gives us in ministry has value in God's plan for people. We must keep an open heart and maintain a proper posture to God at all times so that we may be usable.

In this next chapter, we will see what the Bible teaches on what qualifies someone to be a pastor. The Apostle Peter and the Apostle Paul both give instruction to us as to the high standards required to lead people in the church.

Chapter 1   Defining the Pastor's Role

Study Questions

How do your initial thoughts of what you thought a pastor's role is compare to what we see described in the Bible? What is the difference?

Which leader from the Bible do you most identify with? Whose heart and gifts to you most compare to? Why?

Which leader from the Bible do you least identify with? What heart and gifts do they possess that you feel you like? Why?

When responding to the call of God to be a pastor, are there conditions that you may have before fully obeying God? What are they? Why are they holding you back from full obedience?

Chapter 2

Qualifications of a Pastor

The Bible describes the qualifications for Overseers in the Church. The calling of pastor over people is a high calling by God, and carries much weight with it. With authority comes responsibility. The Apostles, both Peter and Paul share these qualifications of what a faithful pastor should be held to:

Peter

We see the Apostle Peter describe what the standard of pastors are in the Church:

1 Peter 5:2-4
Be shepherds of God's flock that is under your care, watching over them—not because you must, but because you are willing, as God wants you to be; not pursuing dishonest gain, but eager to serve; not lording it over those entrusted to you, but being examples to the flock. And when the Chief Shepherd appears, you will receive the crown of glory that will never fade away.

Peter is describing the heart that a good pastor should have. Your motive must be tested. Your style of leadership must change from what the business world may teach. Peter reveals what I believe is the highest form of leadership – that is, to live as an *example*. Less talk, more walk. Less teaching and more living. As a pastor, you will spend hours a week working on teaching messages for groups in your church. Just as teaching by words is important, all the more is it important that you teach by modeling what you want people to do. Living out your lesson has greater impact than teaching your lesson. But it is much more difficult.

What Are You Pursuing?

The calling of pastor means that you will give up other worldly pursuits. One pursuit I have had to reconcile to give up in my life is the pursuit of wealth and success. I have the natural desire to make money and to feel successful. And while neither are wrong in and of themselves, I have had to lay these pursuits at the altar of the calling God has called me to. To be sure, I should make enough money to provide a comfortable lifestyle for my family. I have always worked on the side to afford some of the extras I want to provide my family. I have been able to pursue some of my own ideas for my personal fulfillment. But I have had to stay focused and stay in my lane of the overarching role that God has me in as pastor.

I remember a couple of years ago I was playing the piano in a restaurant (one of my side jobs). After finishing a three hour music set, I was worn out. I had worked all day at church and gone straight to set up for my evening engagement. As I began to tear down my music equipment, a man came up to me. He had been sitting in the restaurant watching me perform.

The man kindly asked if he could have a word with me. "Sure" I replied.
The man said "I was watching you sing and play tonight and I felt like God wanted me to tell you something. God wanted you to know that He appreciates the extra work you do, so that you could be a pastor in His church."

I was blown away. I had sometimes felt sorry for myself that I had to work a second job to help pay for some of my family's needs or extras that I wanted to provide for them. I was tired from a twelve hour day, and had a busy ministry weekend yet ahead of me. After I packed my gear in my car, I headed home. On the ride home, what the man said hit me, and I began to cry. I felt God had told me "thank you, Matt. I appreciate the sacrifice you are making to serve me."

Being a pastor is more about who you are than what you do. That is such a hard truth to grasp, at least for me. Society encourages an easy life. Culture celebrates wealth, accumulation, and fame. We are conditioned to measure success by trophies and money. God measures success differently.

God celebrates faith and faithfulness

Pastor, I am wanting to break down your conventional thinking. You need to begin to think how God wants you to think. Start looking at God's dashboard of success. It is very different than what you are used to. In many ways, it is exactly opposite of how you approach life. Think of this concept to help you: just like you are starting a new job and want to learn how to please your new boss, you need to understand how to please your new boss – that is God, by the way. He is the One you ultimately answer to.

Faith

Faith will become the foundation on which you think, on which you operate, on which you move forward in your ministry. Faith is hard. Faith takes some courage and some crazy. It is so essential that you embrace faith and live it out on a continual basis as a pastor. Why? Because faith pleases God. You need God's favor! You want Him working for you and with you.

Hebrews 11:6
Without faith, it is impossible to please God

God responds to people who put their faith in Him, in what He says. This has everything to do with being a person of faith. It is a mindset of deep belief. Our actions will follow what our mind is set on. Understand this: whatever we focus our attention on becomes bigger to us. When you focus on your high belief in God, you will find that you will see Him in greater ways than you ever could otherwise. When you focus on what God has said to you, what His Word declares for you, you will see His plan unfold right before your eyes.

To follow Jesus Christ requires faith. We tithe on our income based on faith. Logically, it does not make sense to live on 90% of your income. It takes faith. It does not make sense to come to church every Sunday and serve when you are busy and tired from a long work week. It requires faith. It is not natural to share your life in small groups with other imperfect people in the church so that you can grow. It asks for faith. Just as the Apostle Peter shares in the verse above, you must live out faith in front of others. People follow your faith, not your preaching. They follow your faith, not your success. Faith inspires people like nothing else. Faith causes movement in a church faster than any campaign or sermon could. Your faith is infectious. It is necessary. It is powerful!

Faithfulness

You also need to demonstrate faithfulness. Please do not underestimate how your faithfulness affects your impact as a pastor. While faith inspires, faithfulness establishes. When people see you are faithful to your word, when you are committed to your post as pastor, they begin to trust you. I have seen pastors who honestly did not have much skill in leadership. There were so many pieces they were missing in their tool kit. But they still have a group of people following them. It simply because the pastor had remained faithful to God and faithful to people. You can actually outlast other great leaders, great churches if you will just remain consistent and faithful. Faithfulness is big on God's list of favorites:

> faith inspires, faithfulness establishes

Matthew 25:33
The Master replied: "well done thy good and faithful servant. You have been faithful with a few things. I will be faithful in many things. Come share in your Master's happiness.

This verse shows how faithfulness gets you far in God's Kingdom. Simply staying where God has placed you will pay dividends. This can be difficult when you have been in the same place for a while. Every 7 years, I seem to get the "itch" for something new and exciting. What I have learned is something I call "Staying Power." Great things have happened in my ministry just because I stayed put. I have learned that unless God says GO, I will stay and GROW. Pastor, don't ever get in front of God. Don't ever judge for yourself if YOU think you are done with an assignment. Let God make that call. Remember that God looks at things differently than you do. Trust Him. Live a life of Faith and Faithfulness.

Paul

The Apostle Paul also speaks to the qualifications of a pastor:

1 Timothy 3:1-6
Here is a trustworthy saying: Whoever aspires to be an overseer desires a noble task.
Now the overseer is to be above reproach, faithful to his wife, temperate, self-controlled, respectable, hospitable, able to teach, not given to drunkenness, not violent but gentle, not quarrelsome, not a lover of money. He must manage his own family well and see that his children obey him, and he must do so in a manner worthy of full respect.
(If anyone does not know how to manage his own family, how can he take care of God's church?) He must not be a recent convert, or he may become conceited and fall under the same judgment as the devil.

Leading at Home

Paul teaches a requirement to lead in your home first before try-ing to lead others in the church. This is more difficult and com-plex than it may appear.

The reason this is so important to get right is that the natural pull of a pastor is to people and to their needs. And, as the church grows, there are more ministries, more leaders to coach, more problems to address. Guess what sometimes gets forgotten and neglected? Your family. Your marriage. Your kids.
You must be intentional to schedule time and energy for your family. They MUST come first in your passion, first in your focus.

My wife, Kellie helps me regulate how I am doing with this. And I need constant regulating. One day she confronted me by saying that I would come home exhausted, with nothing left to give. She said that she and our kids were getting my leftovers. That image stuck with me. From that day forward, I shifted my thinking that my family would start getting my BEST, not just the REST.

What Your Family Needs

As you endeavor to lead well in your home, ask the question of yourself, "what does my family need of me?" Sometimes, I come home and still have my "pastor hat" on, barking orders to my "staff" or trying to counsel my family, or teaching the Bible to my family. And while I am to be a pastor in my home, my wife reminds me that what they need from me is "normal dad, normal husband."

The way my wife will approach her relationship with God may look different than others in our church. The way my daughter is involved in the church will look different from my son. One size does not fit all. As a husband and as a dad, I must love them and understand them enough to allow them to have their own, unique journey with God. We should not expect them to keep up with everyone else in the church. Remember that a Shepherd GUIDES, he does not PULL ALONG.

Take a moment and discern if you are having to drag your family to church. Are you always preaching at your family? Are you constantly demanding they go to every church function? From personal experience, I will tell you that dragging them along on their spiritual journey will frustrate them, and will disappoint you. You must relax, give them plenty of space, and love them for who they are. Your life will demonstrate what you want them to follow. People follow the example of their father, not their preaching. Such a harsh truth to realize, but very true. I am working to get better at this. I love my family. I want them to love God and love the church like I do.

A Higher Standard

The Apostle Paul sets the bar high for the pastor. He speaks of self-control in areas of drinking and of emotion. The words he uses are powerful: live ABOVE REPROACH. That infers we should restrict our lifestyle choices to higher pursuits, for the purpose of not putting ourselves in a compromising situation. Is it wrong to drink alcohol? Not according to the Bible. Is it wrong to show anger or frustration? Not when I see examples in the Bible of how to properly show emotion.

However, the idea of living above reproach means that you do not allow yourself to do certain things or cross certain lines for the sake of people who are following you in the church. For every pastor, that line will look different. In my life, I am always trying to draw clear lines, so I create safe guard rails of protection. I create them so I can see them. I create them so my wife can see them. I want my children to recognize them and understand why I have created them, so they will

don't tear down a fence until you know why it was put there

learn from me. And I show my staff and my inner circle families the lines I endeavor to keep and manage in my life.

I was sharing with my parents one day about this concept of building up guardrails. They said they grew up with a wise parable that stated "don't tear down a fence until you know why it was put there." That is wisdom. Guardrails are tools that will protect against danger.

Pastor Todd Mullins of Christ Fellowship taught me a great perspective of drawing lines in our life as leaders in the church. He draws his line a bit farther in the safe zone than it needs to be. Whether it deals with drinking alcohol, watching certain movies, how he interacts with the opposite sex, he decided he will live more protected than others. His philosophy is this: if you would ever cross your own line of accountability, and your line is farther away than what would be considered inappropriate, you would still be far from crossing a more dangerous line. In other words, he does not choose to always live on the edge of compromise. Rather, he is always leaning toward holiness, appropriateness, accountability.

I respect him so much for his intentional lifestyle choices. Because of his example, I have endeavored to restrict myself from the casual so I can embrace the holy. I am far from perfect, but I ave been intentional evaluate where my lines fall, and how I am managing them. My wife helps me, my parents, my Supervisor, and my pastor. Even my friends help me evaluate how I am doing.

What are your lines? Can you list them for me? In what areas of your life have you drawn lines? For the areas that you have not thought of to draw lines, you likely will find some compromise and some areas that are in danger of failing. Who knows the lines that you have drawn? Have you written them down? To be qualified and to STAY qualified as a pastor, you need to make some decisions on what you do and what you do not, and then manage those decisions through accountability of others.

Pastor, you are called of God. But you are vulnerable. You are weak. You are susceptible. The enemy of your soul, Satan does not want you to succeed as a pastor. You are a direct threat to his scheme. You need to draw lines in your life and understand you are in a battle. The Apostle Paul draws a vivid picture of the battle we are in and the readiness we must live in at all times:

Ephesians 6:10-18 NIV
Finally, be strong in the Lord and in his mighty power. Put on the full armor of God, so that you can take your stand against the devil's schemes. For our struggle is not against flesh and blood, but against the rulers, against the authorities, against the powers of this dark world and against the spiritual forces of evil in the heavenly realms.
Therefore put on the full armor of God, so that when the day of evil comes, you may be able to stand your ground, and after you have done everything, to stand. Stand firm then, with the belt of truth buckled around your waist, with the breastplate of righteousness in place, and with your feet fitted with the readiness that comes from the gospel of peace. In addition to all this, take up the shield of faith, with which you can extinguish all the flaming arrows of the evil one. Take the helmet of salvation and the sword of the Spirit, which is the word of God.
And pray in the Spirit on all occasions with all kinds of prayers and requests. With this in mind, be alert and always keep on praying for all the Lord's people.

Conclusion

We see the qualifications of a pastor from both Peter and Paul. The role of a pastor is not to be seen as a career-building opportunity. It is not to achieve success as the world defines it. It is a life of calling and of mission. This holy calling must first be lived out at home. Your spouse and your children are your primary disciples, and you are to lead them BY EXAMPLE, through modeling the life you hope they will catch and live.

In this chapter, we defined the qualities and the responsibilities of a pastor. Our natural response is to begin feeling the weight of responsibility, feeling like we have to esteem to be ALL of these great qualities as leaders and pastors.

In the next chapter, I want to address some of the areas that pastors get stuck when attempting to live up to being the "perfect pastor." As I aim to teach you what I have learned about being a Strategic Pastor, I want you first to be aware of the pitfalls that we all have to navigate through, so we can sustain our calling for the long haul.

Chapter 2   Qualifications of a Pastor

Study Questions

What are your pursuits with regard to your calling as pastor? How do the pursuits that you celebrate match up to what God celebrates?

When assessing your spiritual leadership at home, how would you rate yourself on a scale of 1 to 10? What growth and new practices would help you raise your number rating by 2 points? What new discipline would get you to a 9 or 10?

Because the calling of pastor requires that we live above reproach, in what ways have you decided to hold yourself to a higher standard? In what areas do you know you need to raise your standard so that you can be qualified to be a pastor to people?

Chapter 3

Pitfalls of a Pastor

The reason I felt led to write this book is that I want you to win as a pastor. Whether you are currently a pastor, or you aspire to become a pastor, I want you to not just survive, I want you to thrive.

I have met great people who started with incredible passion and vision. Many have excellent skills and extensive education. However, in a few short years, they grew tired, overwhelmed and became discouraged. The role of pastor is so all-encompassing, so massive in scope, that one could never hope to fulfill all of the expectations people have. Herculean holiness and super-human strength tend to wear out even the most dedicated person, pushing them to burn out or to give up on ministry altogether.

It does not have to end this way for you. There are great examples of people who have sustained long years of effective ministry. We studied some in the Bible in the previous chapter. There are many today we can point to who embody what the Bible qualifies as a pastor.

This book is all about strategies that can help you have great success and lasting fruit from your labor. The first thing I want to do is to address some of the common pitfalls you will be faced with. There are some areas that can trap you and get you stuck in a pit where you will never be able to climb out of. They can disguise themselves as well-intentioned motives and endeavors. But if you are not aware of these pitfalls, you will spend all of your energy trying to climb out, while not charging the mountains that God has called you to take.

Pitfall #1: The Needs

A pastor sees the needs and the opportunities to respond more than any other person in the church. Because most pastors are built with mercy, compassion, and a sensitivity for people, their natural tendency is to respond. Loves responds.

As the pastor of your people and of the church, you will feel the weight of the needs more than anyone else. You may have staff that can help you. You may have some great volunteers that are involved in supporting you. But the "buck stops with you."

Another dynamic you will deal with is that people see you as the Shepherd, the care giver. People look to you for spiritual guidance and Biblical teaching. Some will hold you in higher regard as a leader and authority figure in their life. So naturally, when they are in crisis, they want their pastor to know, and want their pastor to come visit. For you to delegate care would be unthinkable, and the last thing you would want them to feel is that you are uncaring and off-putting. Because of your compassion, you intuitively want to respond, to drop everything and jump in with both feet.

Sometimes, the need is not with a person who contacts you. It is a need they know of. Who do they call? They call you, their pastor. Whether it be someone who is homeless, or an opportunity to help a family whose car won't start, the person calling you thinks that this would be the PERFECT opportunity for "the church" to do something. And, when they finish with you, it is like they are dumping the need in your lap:

"Pastor, will you call them?"
"Pastor, can our church make an announcement this Sunday and take a collection?"

"Pastor, can a group of men go over and fix that lady's car?"

The problem with this is that if you, the pastor are spending so much energy in meeting the needs of the people, you are not able to spiritually lead your church. You cannot be hunched over being attentive to the people, going from hospital to home, to counseling appointment to your office, and then get up on the platform on Sunday to spiritually lead your church.

When people bombard you with opportunities to serve others and solve problems, you find that you are chasing their priorities, their ideas. Deep beneath the surface, you will become frustrated. Why? Because you are not personally attached to this need; God did not put this in your heart to do. You are solving a problem *they* brought to you. You are responding to a need *they* saw. Your days are spent trying to get your volunteers motivated to respond to a need that is not even your vision. Brian Tracy, motivational speaker says Brian Tracy, motivational speaker says "if you do not have a plan for your day, someone else will!" How true.

> "if you do not have a plan for your day, someone else will!"
> Brian Tracy

The challenge of being the pastor is that you must wear many hats. You must wear the hat of:

- Leader
- Teacher
- Financial Officer
- Coach
- Celebrator
- Boss
- Spiritual Warrior
- Care Giver
- Team Builder

...And I've got a lot more I could add...

To manage all of the hats, you must learn to distribute how much time and energy you give to care for the needs of the church.

Pastors get stuck here because they struggle with self-regulating how they are doing in controlling the percentage of their time, energy and focus. Most pastors thrive in the area of care and compassion, so they feel they should drop everything and respond to every need. But your care of people and your response to the needs presented **needs to be strategic.**

Should you prioritize people's needs? It depends. Should you drop everything when someone is in crisis? It depends. Should you commit to take on opportunities presented to you by others? It depends.

There is A LOT I could give you on the subject of care. A lot. But to stay concise, I will just give you a few nuggets that will help you get unstuck from the pitfall of trying to care for everyone and everything.

Love Unconditionally, Invest Strategically

Dr. Tom Mullins, Founding Pastor of Christ Fellowship church in South Florida taught me this:

Love everyone unconditionally, but invest yourself strategically.

I love the heart of this, and I love the wisdom behind it. This axiom frees us from guilt of being selective in who and how we invest in to people. This gives us permission to be "unfair" with our time and energy.

I live this principle out by loving and caring for all people in the church on Sunday mornings and Wednesday nights. That is when I am with the most people in my church, so I maximize those moments. When someone says "Pastor, I want to get with you this week to share something" I respond with "I've got a few minutes now, what is on your mind?" I can address their idea or concern right there. When someone feels they need to share for a long time, I kindly interrupt them by caring for them and offer to pray for them right there. You can do a lot in a short moment, and can touch the need they have if you lead the moment.

To stay balanced in my time with people, I want to share with you some of the boundaries I have learned to set for myself. Keeping within these principled boundaries help me avoid falling into the pit of reacting to people's needs all of the time. To stay within the Biblical vain, I like to describe them as my "Thou Shall Nots". Very Charlton Heston. If you do not understand the reference, look it up.

Thou Shall Not...

Thou Shall Not Counsel

I do not counsel. Period. When people are looking for extensive time with me with a personal issue, I tell them I am not a trained counselor. I explain to them I am a pastor who loves them, who wants to support them and who wants to help them grow in their walk with Jesus.

I will give people Biblical teaching and wisdom in to their situation. I will care for people in their moment of need and encourage them. But I do not allow long sessions with people, and I do not have ongoing meetings. My rule is that I will meet with anybody once. However, I am selective in how I will meet with them. I can meet the needs of most people on Sunday mornings around our church service times. Some meetings may need more focused time, and I will schedule those around Wednesday night ministries. My midweek meetings are restricted to mostly leaders who I want to invest strategic time. These are the key people that are carrying the weight of leadership and responsibility with me for the church.

> If you care well for your leaders , they will care well for the church.

Build a team and a system where you can appropriately address the needs of your church. If you care well for your leaders, they will care well for the church people.

As a Strategic Pastor, you must protect your time. Love everyone with great care, but be strategic in how you display care. Care through others.

Thou Shall Not Return Calls

The conventional rule in the professional world suggests that every phone call should be responded to within twenty-four hours. But with the advent of texting, e-mail, and with the ability for people to message you on Social Media platforms, I suggest that it is unrealistic to keep this twenty-four hour rule of response.

Consider this: people can have access to you 52 times a year by attending weekend church services. If you include a mid- week ministry night, that adds up to over 100 times a year that you are making yourself available. When you put this in perspective, you soon begin to realize that it is not necessary, nor healthy for you to have to respond to every call or message that hits your computer or phone.

I listen to all voice mails and read all messages I receive. But I do not try to read them immediately, and I certainly do not respond to all of them. I look for people who I owe my response to, which is my boss, my family, and my key families and leaders. When there is a family in my church who I have close relationship to, I respond to their need. But many messages are not urgent and some not important.

How do you deal with the people who you do not return their call or request? What I find is that if it is important to them, they will find me at church and ask me about it. If they seem disappointed that I did return their call, I don't try to explain or make an excuse. I redirect the conversation and offer to meet their need there in the moment. It is there where I can give them more attention and care in person. I have found that people accept that from me.

The great thing is that by doing this, I have trained people how they can access me. Now, I get fewer calls and messages during the week and people are not disappointed with me because they have learned how to interact with me! You can do the same.

Thou Shall Not know every person

When your church grows beyond ne hundred people, you will struggle with maintaining a deep relationship with every person. I remember when our Stuart Campus grew to three hundred people, I thought I could build a friendship with every single person. I am relational by nature, so I would instinctively extend myself to all three hundred people that were a part of our church. When new people would come, I would attempt to make them my new friend. However, I could not keep up. I wore out in my first six months trying to be everybody's friend and personal pastor.

I remember walking up and down the aisles in church services trying to pour in to every relationship. I would over-commit myself by offering to have lunch or coffee with many people. The problem is, I would forget to write some of these appointments down and would forget I had made commitments. I disappointed some people when in the next few weeks, I had not called to follow through.

What I had to learn was that I cannot be close to everybody. I cannot have that close friendship with every person who comes to my church. I began to realize the importance of developing leaders and pastors around me who could help carry the load of building relationships. I understood the dynamic that everyone wants to know the pastor and be known by the pastor. My friend and fellow pastor, Travis O'Neal says "there is no one like the pastor who can connect with people." He is right. So, this made me transfer my leadership to some trusted people who had the gift of pastoring people. They would extend my heart and my face. More on this in my chapter on developing leaders.

As a Strategic Pastor, you must love all people unconditionally, and be accessible to everyone - but only at strategic high-people times. Invest yourself strategically during the low people times. Build space in your week to be alone so you can evaluate, prepare, and sharpen yourself. Meet only with people who add to you and are ready to help you lead the mission of the church. In later chapters, I will tell you who these people are and how to invite them in to your Inner Circle.

Now that I have shared my "Thou Shall Nots", I want to give you my "Thou Shalls", the principles I practice in attending to all of the needs of the people. This is how I love everyone unconditionally, but keep investing strategically for high impact.

Thou Shall...

Thou Shall Leave Empty Handed

This principle will change your life. With every interaction you have with people who come to you for direction or help, place the responsibility for action ON THEM. Always give THEM the resources and have THEM follow up with you. Never leave the interaction with steps you must take. Leave every interaction *empty-handed.* Remember that you are being confronted with many people every day – at the restaurant, in your neighborhood, at church, dropping your kids off at school. If you think that you can take everything that people put on you, you are going to topple over with the load of work. Your shoulders were not meant to carry so much weight!.

This principle demands that you create systems within your church where you can re-direct people who approach you. See how in the First Century church, the Leaders built a team and system to meet the needs of the people:

Acts 6:2-4 NLT
...the Twelve called a meeting of all the believers. They said, "We apostles should spend our time teaching the word of God, not running a food program. And so, brothers, select seven men who are well respected and are full of the Spirit and wisdom. We will give

them this responsibility. Then we apostles can spend our time in prayer and teaching the word."

You cannot just ignore problems, I know. You cannot let people hang out to do ministry with no help or direction, I understand. But you must put the responsibility back on them. Help them find the solution. Challenge them to be the solution. When you solve

> When you solve their problem, you teach them that you are the answer. When you teach them how to solve the problem, you empower them to find the answer.

their problem, you teach them that you are the answer. When you teach them how to solve the problem, you empower them to find the answer.

Thou Shall Sympathize, Not Empathize

Sympathy and Empathy are similar. They even sound similar. But to avoid the pitfall of becoming stuck in every need or crisis, you need to *sympathize* more than empathize.

What's the difference? Sympathize is to feel the pain of another person. Empathize is to actually TAKE ON the pain of another person. Sympathy suggests more of a separation from people's pain and needs. To stay healthy and to keep balance as the pastor, you need to create separation from people's pain and challenges. As the Leader of the church, you must stay focused on leading the church. As a person, you must stay healthy so you can be an example to the church.

To remind myself of this, I have to say a powerful statement to myself many times:

God, you are God. I am not.
Repeat that right now 3 times, then have some chocolate, just to treat yourself.

As pastors, we put too much pressure on ourselves to solve people's problems so we can ease their pain. We cannot solve every problem, and we cannot take away every pain. You cannot sustain hurt and pain day after day and remain healthy. You do not deserve that, and your family does not deserve the dysfunction you inadvertently bring home with you from ministry.

One friend of mine is a Christian Counselor. I asked her how she stays emotionally healthy after dealing with people's hurts and struggles day after day. She says that she practices a skill that helps her. As soon as the person walks out of her office after a counseling session, she pretends that their problems walk right out with them. She said she had to learn this skill because she would go home all night worrying about the person's problems, causing her to be depressed and miserable. She found that the person came back the next week doing fine because they had moved on, but she, the Counselor had been stewing all week over the pain and struggle of her patient!

Sympathize, don't empathize

Thou Shall Have a Plan

As a pastor, you are in the people business. You are all about loving and serving people. When people come with their needs, what is your plan to respond? Are you prepared if one hundred people come to you at once needing gas money? What happens if five people are in the hospital, while five others have passed away, all in the same week?

Since you are in the people business, you need a system as to how your church responds to people. When people ask for money or for help, you should already have a policy in place of what amount you can give, and who gets help. Listen to me. It is alright to not help some people. It is alright not to be everybody's solution. It is appropriate not to have the church open and accessible for any person to just stop over when they feel like it.

Take the pressure off of yourself to have to make hard decisions in the moment every time a need pops up. This puts pressure on you and your team when a decision must be made. There is something called decision fatigue that is very real and has been studied at Columbia University. It shows that throughout a work day, we get tired of having to exert mental and emotional energy in having to make so many decisions. By the end of the day, we tend to make poor decisions. Not having a strategic plan in place will result in poor decisions for you and your church.

Every person's need is different, and interacting with people will take energy and consideration. Take time with your team to create some policies and clarity as to how you will respond to people. This will take the guilt and stress away, and will help your church feel like it is effectively meeting the needs that come.

Pitfall #2: The Vision

Pastors understand that they have the responsibility and the privilege to bring the vision to the church. However, most visions are too ambiguous and too far reaching. How many churches have you seen have a vision that is going to "reach the world?" Or "rescue the lost?"

Pastors can get stuck in what I call "vision mode". They can always be vision-minded, but never take any specific steps towards seeing the vision become reality. Usually, the problem is that they are reaching for the clouds when they need to reach for what is right in front of them.

Dream Big, Start Small

Big dreams are great. God-sized vision is what you need. God has called your church to have great impact, and He wants to provide all that you need to accomplish your calling. But practically speaking you need to learn to dream big, but start small. My dad once coached me when I was sharing my big vision with him, of all of the grand things I thought God wanted me to expand out and do. After I was done with all of my grandiose ideas, he said "God's will for your life is to take care of today. If you will do what you need to do today, then God will get you where you need to be tomorrow. That is God's will."

If you will take action on the clear steps in front of you today, then God will prepare the next steps for you tomorrow. God will get you where He is calling you. That's how you get unstuck from the nebulous vision mode. Be faithful with today, and take one step at a time.

An Untested Vision

For you, the vision is likely the most exciting part of the church. It is what captured your heart and mind to step in to the calling of pastor. I talk to so many men and women who share with me their "God-calling" story. Their eyes light up. Their voice inflects excitement. Their body language is leaning in. I love it. I have that same passion and I love to see it manifest in people.

The tricky part is to define what the vision is, or, rather, what it should be.

Birthing a vision is likely much like birthing a baby. You pray for your baby, watch him grow, and witness him come in to the world. You are so proud of your baby. You fall in love with him. You see yourself through their little eyes. Your baby is a gift from God.

As a new parent, you become protective of our baby. You are sensitive if anyone would say a critical word about our baby. It is beautiful and delicate and special - leave him alone!

Our vision is truly a gift of God, much like having a baby. We have seen it incubate in the womb of our spirit and now it is coming to life. We are proud of it. This is as it should be. You are the spiritual parent of your vision. You are to look after it, and to see it grow to its full potential.

What I am suggesting however is to take one step back from your vision and become more objective about it. A great vision must be tested. If the vision is ever going to mature and become what it was meant to be, you must allow it to go through the painful growth process.

The first step in testing you vision is to ask refining questions:
What are the problems in the world today?
What is God's purpose for people?
How is our Church fulfilling that purpose?
How can people live out our vision?
Is the vision specific?
Will the vision help people in a way that they will appreciate?

If your vision has not been put through the refining process of answering questions like this, then it is untested. It is pie in the sky. Your vision may look great on paper, but will have little chance of surviving. Don't hold on too tightly to your "baby vision." It may be that you need to take more time and bring other people in to the prayer process with you to help you forge a greater and more relevant vision for your church.

A Blurry Vision

Vision is fuzzy. Most people love the idea of a vision because it engages their hearts and minds. But vision can mean different things to different people. The problem with vision is that everyone sees differently. Therefore, many visions can emerge.

When the vision is blurry, the people can get confused, disillusioned, and even frustrated. Solomon wrote about what happens to people without a clear and compelling vision:

Proverbs 29:18
Where there is no vision, the people cast off restraint.

People tend to want to go their own way. Strong-minded people will quickly come up with their own version of what the church's vision should be. That is why to avoid the vision pitfall, you must take great care to articulate the vision so that it paints a picture of a better tomorrow for the people. You must communicate it effectively and share it consistently with everyone. Only then, when people digest the vision and embrace it as their own will they unify for the sake of reaching the vision.

Understand this principle: before they buy in to the vision, they first must buy in to you , their pastor. This demands that you live a life of integrity, passion, commitment and leadership that will attract people to hear what you have to say about vision and direction.

> **Before they buy in to the vision, they first must buy in to you**

Pitfall #3: The Ministries

What ministries do your church offer? Really, the question to ask is, what ministries DON'T you offer?

Another pitfall for pastors is that we try to do too much. This is a tendency in our personal lives, and it manifests in the church. Tommy Barnett, pastor of First Assembly of God in Arizona taught the mindset for ministry "when you see a need, fill it." That is such a great principle, and I embrace it. One of the best ways to discern what ministries your church will offer is to get out in your community and see what the greatest needs are. When your church begins to solve the problems within the community, they will see your church as an answer to the community. People are attracted to churches that are effective and are on mission.

The pitfall here is that it's easy to start a new ministry, but it's hard to sustain it. It's exciting to add. It's difficult to subtract. Painful, actually.

In the book, Essentialism, Author Greg McKeown teaches the principal of doing less so that you can produce more. He speaks of focus and intentionality. The author teaches an object lesson by directing us to go in to our closest and purge twenty percent of our wardrobe. When we assess what clothes we want to keep, we begin to evaluate the clothes we do not wear much, if at all. Once we finish with this exercise, we will feel better emotionally knowing that we have created more space in our closet. McKeown challenges us to practice this every year in our closet. (I tried this. It felt great!)

This pruning principle is rarely practiced in the church, yet it would yield much fruit. You see, the pitfall that traps us is that once new ministries are started, the pastor must expend his energy to sustain the excitement to keep people engaged in that ministry. When you start a food pantry for the homeless, many volunteers come the first Saturday morning. But the next Saturday, far less come. You and the faithful few are left doing all of the work. When you start a mentoring program for under-privileged kids, the resources needed to teach and care for them become costly and pull from other ministries.

I remember when we started Stuart Campus for Christ Fellowship in 2007. We had a difficult time finding a venue in Martin County that would work to launch a church. Our last hope was Martin County High School, the oldest school in the region. To win over the school, we tried to find small ways to add value to the school. We fed the teachers lunch. We cleaned up the school. We mowed their grass. And we agreed to remodel the foyer of the auditorium that we would use for our sanctuary.

I remember on our first Saturday, we had many volunteers there to clean, remodel and paint in the foyer. We had enough volunteers that one of my leaders started having people paint inside the auditorium. That task was not something we had originally agreed to do. My leader had several people rolling paint on walls in that large auditorium with a high ceiling. I remember questioning my leader, but she said "we have more than enough people." Actually, I was excited to see our church taking on such a monumental task, and I loved seeing our people serve the school.

However, the next week, we had less than half the amount of volunteers show up. We finished about 75 % of the room. The third week, we had five volunteers ready to paint and finished 95

% of the room after a long day, just leaving the very highest and most difficult spots to paint. We did not have the high ladders to reach those spots, but they were obvious to see. I was panicking. If I did not get that room finished and looking professional, the school would be mad and our church would look bad. I desperately called men in our church until I got one man who had a tall ladder and was willing to help me finish the project. We came in on a Saturday morning and spent hours working together to reach those high places to paint and finish. I was worn out by the experience and vowed I would never paint again.

When you say yes to one thing, get ready to say yes to several more things.

Ask Great Questions

To avoid the ministry pitfall, you need to start with asking good questions:

What are the needs of our community?
What is the greatest need?
What are we equipped to do best?
What are we called to do as a church?
As the pastor, where do my passions lie?
What are the passions of some of my greatest leaders and families?
What one ministry will be known for in our community?
What will we choose not to do?
What will help our church grow healthy and stay on mission?

There are a dozen other questions you could and should ask. You must become selective in choosing the ministries you offer. If you are starting a church, this becomes easier because you do not have to prune anything or stop anything. If you are the pastor of an established church, this becomes difficult and delicate. Yet, pruning is a necessary part of the growth process. Jesus pruned and He even removed! See this example in Scripture:

Mark 12:12-14
The next day as they were leaving Bethany, Jesus was hungry. Seeing in the distance a fig tree in leaf, he went to find out if it had any fruit. When he reached it, he found nothing but leaves, because it was not the season for figs. Then he said to the tree, "May no one ever eat fruit from you again." And his disciples heard him say it.

Find your Focus

> **When everything is important, nothing is important.**

You need to remain realistic. You have limited time, energy, and resources. You cannot make everything important. When everything is important, nothing is important. It all just becomes noise.

You cannot lead people to do many things. As the pastor, you need to find your focus. You need to define it. If you are like me, you will need help with this. Get a team of strategists, creatives, and thinkers around you. Invite them in to this conversation. When you are open-handed with selecting the ministries that your church will offer, you will endear a team around you who will help support the rational for your decision process.

Rather than seeing your church as a hospital that responds to every need you see, think more like a business that has a specific product that it offers. Starbucks is known for their coffee. Lexus is known for their cars. What is your church known for? What does your church provide that brings great value to others?

If your church feels more like a hospital, you will always be *reacting* to people's needs and wants. A Business mindset focuses you to *respond* with what you are and what you have to offer. Both can serve the community. Both can meet the needs that you identify. But one will *paralyze* you, while the other will *propel* you to greater reach and effectiveness.

The Right Fit

When considering what ministries you will offer, you must assess what capacity you have. What resources do you have currently? What facilities do you possess? These pieces will dictate what ministries you can or should offer, and will restrict you from what you should not offer, at least not yet.

astors who have great ideas and vision sometimes try to offer more than they are ready for. Their eyes are bigger than their capacity. While it is great to think big, not small, you want to make sure you do everything with excellence. If you cannot do it well, then you should not do it.

Pastor Tom Mullins teaches: *Excellence honors God and inspires others*

What I am suggesting is that you scale down the ministry that you wish to offer to the size, scope and capacity that your church is positioned to offer. You can do small well. You can do simple with excellence.

I have seen church worship teams have a choir, but there were only 10 people singing. I have witnessed a band, who only had a keyboard player and a drummer. Both did not sound or look that good. The people in the groups were passionate. But their presentation was rough. They were not helping anybody in the church connect to God. It showed great effort, but did not bring excellence.

If your church does not yet have a music program built up to where it can pull off a choir and band, I would suggest you start over. Start by getting with your singers and musicians as a team and be honest with them. With love and respect, show them where they are at as a church, and show them a better vision. You likely need to re-direct them to serve in a more appropriate, more effective place in the church. Start scouting for one or two talented singers and musicians and re-stage the worship ministry with a culturally relevant look and sound. Better to have excellent worship presentation with one or two people doing an acoustic set every Sunday, than to try to present a choir and band that will not be excellent.

Apply this to every area of your church, with every ministry you provide:

How can you scale down the ministry to the stage of life of the church?
How can you scale down how much your ministry will produce?
Does the ministry have to meet every week? Or can it meet once a quarter?
Can the ministry be a one-time event, rather than be ongoing?
What if your Home Group strategy was to challenge everyone to commit to a group for just 4 weeks, rather than expect groups to meet ongoing?

Just like we need to have a reality check with trying to wear clothes that no longer fit us, we need to be honest in our ministries and ask the question "do we have the right fit with the ministries we are trying to provide?"

Conclusion

Even the best, well-meaning pastors are susceptible to falling in the pitfalls surrounding them at every turn. Because you are built to love and respond, you must remain aware of the arduous journey forward to lead your church. Use discretion and guard yourself well. Surround yourself with trusted and proven people who know your blind spots and your tendencies. Empower them to speak in to your leadership and help you navigate the ministry you endeavor to provide.

This next chapter will help you. I believe it will literally change your ministry. It did mine. I am so excited to share this next piece with you, because I believe it is the secret to becoming a Strategic Pastor.

As I have said before, I do not want you to just survive as a pastor. I want you to thrive. To thrive, you need a great strategy. You need to become clear on what you are spending your time and energy on. A common theme in this book is to not just work hard, but to work smart.

As a Strategic Pastor, you will need to embrace the fact that you have limited time, energy, and resources. Therefore, you should not squander them anywhere and everywhere. You should focus them and leverage them for the greatest impact. As a pastor, you are called to have great impact. Learning this strategy will ensure you enjoy lasting impact.

Chapter 3   Pitfalls of a Pastor

Study Questions

When you see the needs of people within your church, what is the tendency that you most struggle with? Why? What is the root cause of your response?

With the pitfall of vision, what will be your biggest tendency that you know about yourself? What have others told you? If you do not know what others say, you may have a bigger problem. Ask three people who know you about how you deal with vision. Ask two people who are allies, and one person who you would consider opposing you. Learn from them.

With the pitfall of ministries that you offer, or that you hope to offer, what has been your pruning process to decide what ministries you should do? Do a quick evaluation right now of what ministries you offer, either as a whole church, or maybe simply within the ministry that you look after within your church. If you cannot list them on paper clearly and logically within three minutes, you likely have fallen deep into the pitfall of too many ministries.

Chapter 4

Triple Threat Process for Strategic Pastors

"Efficiency is doing the thing right. Effectiveness is doing the right thing."
Peter Drucker

All of us want to be effective as a pastor. Trying to keep up with the demands of people and ministry will keep you from being as effective as you would hope to be.

I think most of us show up to the church office every day with a mail box full of e-mails and a list of follow up tasks. Not too much time will pass in the day before we are interrupted by people with problems, ideas and needs of their own. They come looking for us, seeking answers and time. After we have met everyone's needs, the last that thing that gets our energy are the ministry objectives we know will help our church move to greater effectiveness.

What are you trying to accomplish as the pastor?

This is a difficult question to answer. Previously, we have studied what a pastor is and what he does. It seems that a pastor must be so many things in order to fulfill the Biblical role for the church.

When I show up to the church, I realize there are a lot of roles I could play that would be appropriate. There are many hats I must wear at different times as needed to care for the needs of the church.

The quandary is in knowing what hat should I wear, and when to wear it? I know I should spend time with people. I could be working on a message. I could be managing the church finances. Which should I focus on today?

While we need to tend to all aspects of the church, we need to focus on the work that produces the most effective results. We need a simple game plan that we can practice and master that yields the right kind of work. Like Peter Drucker said, we want to focus not just on *doing things right*. We want to focus on *doing the right thing*. If we *do the right thing*, we will be able to accomplish ALL that our church is called to do.

I have formed a three step process that has brought me great impact in my leadership in the church. I love the game of basketball, so I came up with a basketball analogy. I call this my Triple Threat Process for Pastors. In basketball, when a player has the ball in his hands and is being defended by the opposing team, he becomes most effective when he gets in the triple threat position. He could pass, dribble, or shoot. He becomes a better threat to score with his team when he can do any one of these things in the game, throwing the defense off by always keeping them guessing. In church ministry, I want to teach you my Triple Threat Process that will help you become a highly effective, Strategic Pastor.

I did not come up this in one sitting – I am not naturally strategic. I am people-oriented. The Triple Threat Process came to me as I was analyzing what I do naturally, after I noticed that I was beginning to have great results as a pastor. I was seeing people grow. I was seeing the church grow. And I was seeing leaders on my team promoted to greater roles in the church. I asked myself "what have I been doing these last couple of years?" What I discovered was that I was focusing my energy in three specific tasks:

– Love People

– Build Teams

– Develop Leaders

If you will focus your mind and direct your energy to accomplishing the Triple Threat Process, you will begin to thrive as a pastor. Notice that this does not touch on public speaking, managing tasks, or doing ministry. The Triple Threat Process focuses on people, specifically, the people in your church.

This process must be practiced in the order listed. You do not start by developing leaders so that you can then love people. It must start with the first objective of loving people, which will lead naturally to the second, which is to building teams, and so on.

While I still schedule time to manage other aspects of the church, I spend *most* of my time operating in the Triple Threat Process. And the more the church grows, the more I restrict my energy to doing just these three things. One of the secrets to being a Strategic Pastor is to ask yourself the question "what is it that I can do that no one else can do?" Everything else that needs attention I look to delegate to trusted people. In the beginning of learning to incorporate the Triple Threat Process, you will likely not have many you can delegate all of your work and responsibility to. This dilemma is exactly why you need to start practicing the principles of the Triple Threat Process. You will see that it will begin to free you from being overwhelmed with the load of responsibility and needs.

Triple Threat Step #1 :

Love People

 I shared in the introduction the "Love Chapter" found in First Corinthians describing the essence of Godly love. A pastor must have this type of love for people. God is love, and the foundation of everything we do as a pastor must be grounded in love.

A foundational principle of leadership is that people must feel you love them before they will follow you. They must see that you believe in them. They must sense that your motive is simply to help them grow and become all that God wants to them be.

How can you love people more effectively? How can you prove your love? First Corinthians Chapter 13 shows the great lengths that love goes to prove itself. I want to show you ways you can prove your love practically to people in your church.

Know Them

Loving means knowing. You cannot love someone that you do not know. To know someone implies that you will need to spend time with them. What people want from their pastor more than anything else is their time. Your time and attention is the greatest gift you can give your people.

In leadership, there are many skills you can master, many tasks you can delegate. But in this first and most important piece, you cannot delegate. You cannot short-change people in this area. As a matter of fact, if they sense you are in a rush, your time investment will actually have a negative effect on them. People forget what you said, but they remember how you made them feel. When you are meeting with people, slow down, pay attention, listen well and be present in the moment.

To know people, you must learn their name. Learn their family's names. Find out where they are from, what they do for a living. What are they passionate about? What is important to them? Why? When you can come in to contact with someone you met recently and repeat a detail that you learned about them, you know you have done well. They will be blown away that you were paying attention, that you cared.

What I just described is a tall order! How on earth can we retrieve all of that information? A pastor will talk with many people through the week, and many on Sunday morning. Is it possible to retain people's information when meeting so many?

To effectively learn people's names and information, I have a trick for you. I call it a PEOPLE LIST. I learned this from a mentor, a pastor names Steve Helms. He was one of the pastors who first helped me turn the corner moving from musician to pastor. He told me that every time I came to church, I should always carry two items with me in my pocket:

A pen
A notepad

Pastor Steve gave me an assignment to meet all people in our church who lived in Martin and St. Lucie Counties. Because I was soon to launch Christ Fellowship campus north of the main Palm Beach Gardens Campus, I needed to recruit many families to go with me to launch our first Northern Campus in Martin County. Every time I met people, I was to ask "leading questions" with the goal of identifying those who lived in those Northern Counties. When I found somebody in those regions, I would pull out my pen and notepad and capture their information. To avoid looking overt, I would wait until I said goodbye with the family I met, then would go find a corner in the church building and write down my notes:

- **Names**
- **Phone number**
- **County**

- Details of the family
- How long they have been a part of the church Kids?
- What their passions and gifts are

Sometimes, because I could not remember details like phone numbers, e-mail addresses, I would just pull out the notepad right in front of them, looking embarrassed. However, I found that people were actually flattered that I wanted their information. I was the young pastor who was getting ready to launch a new church. This was exciting to people, and I was asking them to join the team. I found that people were exhilarated, and they were honored that I valued them enough to learn their names, ask about their life, and learn their passions and gifts. People would freely give me their information and ask me to call them.

Later that week, I was able to follow up with them and get them connected on our team. Every week, I began building up my PEOPLE LIST. When I began forming the church teams for our new campus launch, I had 75 names collected and was able to place people strategically so that every ministry had leaders and volunteers.

To this day, I still keep a PEOPLE LIST. Do I do this for the purpose of recruiting? Absolutely. Unashamedly. However, the main purpose is not transactional. It is relational. You see, before I recruit anyone to join our volunteer team, I first take time to know them. Many people who I put on my people list do not necessarily become a volunteer or a financial donor. They may be in the future. But that is not my motive. That is entirely up to them. My goal is to know their name, know their story, their passion. I want them to know that I know them. When I pull out my smart phone and ask for their information, it communicates they are important to me. I ask for their information ONLY AFTER I have had a meaningful interaction with them. The reason I try to capture as many names as possible is that I want to be able to retrieve their information at a moment's notice. It does no good to be sitting in your office thinking about someone great you met on Sunday, but you can't recall their name, or can't contact them because you do not have their information. How great would it be to send a quick text in a couple of weeks saying you loved meeting them and are praying for them? How wonderful if you could gather a few new families together for lunch on a Sunday after church? I do these things all the time. As a result, these people feel known, they feel loved, and they make our church their church home.

One hour I block every week is what I call my PEOPLE HOUR. My PEOPLE HOUR is directly linked to my PEOPLE LIST. My PEOPLE LIST is messy, full of notes and fragmented sentences on my Smart phone. I take a moment to organize my notes so I can easily retrieve them in the future. While I do not try to follow up with every person, I ask the Holy Spirit to direct me to the people I should follow up with. I also print a list of every person in the church who took time to fill out a contact card. I personally call visitors from that report. Some people I contact I do not actually hear back from. I leave a voice message. However, I know that my contact still had value because when they hear my message, or see my text or e-mail, they think "wow – the pastor called me. He did not want anything from me. He just wanted to tell me that he enjoyed meeting me and hopes I come back." That makes people feel loved and valued. That makes your growing church feel small.

Family Portrait

To love your people well means that you are trying to paint yourself in the family portrait of their life. A friend and strategic thinker, Kadi Cole created this image for me, and it is such a beautiful picture of how to love people well. If people look through their life and see you in the most beautiful and even most difficult times of their life, you are in their family portrait.

When they are expecting a new baby, you celebrate with them. When their daughter is graduating college, you brag on them. When tragedy strikes, maybe with finding out a family member has cancer, you take time to reach out with care and support. When you hear that a couple is separated with marriage problems, you call the husband and make sure the wife is contacted as well.

Now, this sounds like I am double-speaking from my teaching of how to limit your caring for everyone. I know, I know. But there is a key principle I practice that allows me to accomplish loving people well:

First Responder

When someone within my church family is dealing with a difficult tragedy, I reach out immediately with a text or a call. Depending on the severity of the situation, I will offer to personally visit them. I see myself as the first responder in our church. Though I have a team of care givers in the church who do much of the care for our church family, I take on the personal responsibility to be the first voice someone hears, the first person to show care and support.

Responding well requires that you stay present in the moment. When you are with them in person, do not be on your cell phone, and do not look rushed. Keep eye contact, be dressed professionally when you arrive, and be attentive to what they need. Gauge the tone of the moment. If someone needs to talk, let them talk and you listen. If someone has no words, you may need to speak for them with words of comfort. Sure, sharing a scripture verse and then praying is always appreciated. But the real impact that you have is in responding, and responding quickly.

I cannot over emphasize this first crucial step of loving people. Love is felt. Love is the foundation. While you will move to the strategies of the next steps, you must ALWAYS give time and heart to the first. A politician once said "it is not enough to do good; you must be SEEN doing good." The same is true for a pastor. It is not good enough to say you love them. You must also *demonstrate* your love for them.

> When your people sense your love for them, they will become more willing to follow you.

When your people sense your love for them, they will become more willing to follow you. Though there are different styles of leadership and different personalities that each of us have, this principle of loving people well is foundational. It is absolutely necessary. A pastor can have all of the strategy and giftings and work ethic in the world, but fail to gain momentum in his calling to lead people in the church without love. Adversely, a pastor may struggle with leadership skills, or not possess strong giftings, but yet still have people that follow him faithfully. This happens as the pastor loves his people well as I have described.

Bob Goff says that love trumps vision every time. I think he is right. Vision is important. But people follow leaders they love and who they trust.

When you love people well, more people will come to your church. You will see growth. Love grows. Love is attractional. So then, what do you do when you have more people to love and care for? What now? How do you manage all of those relationships? How do you make everyone feel special and known? Well, that is why I am writing this book, pastor. These next two steps are how you will keep the love flowing to all of your people.

Triple Threat Process #2:

Build Teams

This second step is my favorite. I think because I am a builder by nature. I am a maximizer. I like to take something that is good and make it better. I like to take something that is average and make it great. And because I am people-oriented, I see people as the greatest resource I have around me. I am a big fan of John Maxwell  and have studied many of his books. I think why I am so drawn to him is that I may be built similar to him. I have the same drive, the same high believe, and the same love for people that he does.

Because I see people before I see anything else, I am baffled at pastors who are stuck doing all of the work, overwhelmed with responsibility and having no church growth. I want to tell them "don't you see everyone standing around watching you work, wail and whine?"

Three people can walk into the same room and see three different things. The first can see that the chairs are not aligned in order. The second can see that the colors of the room do not match. The third sees the people in the room. If you are process-oriented, you want to go fix the chairs. If you are environment-oriented, you want to go to the store and purchase décor that will make the room match. If you are people-oriented, you will begin connecting with people.

I want to challenge you to become people-oriented. Here is why. First, because God loves people more than anything. Second, because people are your greatest resource. Pastor, it is not your preaching that will grow the church. It is not your platform or music presentation that is your greatest resource. It is not even your budget or facility that is your greatest resource.

The way you are going to accomplish all that you are called to do as the pastor is to mobilize the people to BE the church. The way you are going to see church growth and health is by building teams around you to accomplish the mission. I want to instill a concept that will help you see people as they could be within your church.

I want to show you how I build teams around me.

> The way you are going to accomplish all that you are called to do as the pastor is to mobilize the people to BE the church.

People = Team

Think sports. Most people like sports. And when people think sports, they begin to grasp a team concept. Sports tend to get people fired up. Sports are goal-oriented. Every team wants to win the game. Every team sees themselves as champions. A team works together to rise above a challenge. Working toward a challenge can bring out greatness in people. There is so much that can be learned by studying the attributes of a winning team.

People want to belong to a team, a winning team. The number one need of people is to feel they belong. This speaks to significance. We want to matter. We want to fulfill our purpose on this earth. Yet too many pastors are focused on their own significance and their own ministry that they are unaware of this vital need embedded in their people.

I love basketball. I am not very good at it, but I enjoy it, nevertheless. My son is only 14 years old, and he is already beating me... and I don't let him win easily. One thing I love about basketball is watching players who make the other players better. The greatest point guards dribble the ball while keeping their head up. They are looking for openings to pass the ball to their teammates so that they can score a goal. I heard a Sports Commentator yell after a great pass and score play "when you pass the ball, everybody eats!" The best players play basketball remembering that it is a team sport. In order to win consistently, the team has to win, not just the individual.

As the pastor, you need to become a Team Coach. You need to start scouting for potential great players that can join your team. You are not the player, you are the Coach. The Coach does not play basketball on the court with his team. He remains on the sidelines and he lets the team play the game. Most pastors are guilty of trying to score the points, playing defense and pulling down rebounds. The rest of the team is watching from the sidelines. No one wants to play with a ball hog, even if the ball hog is the greatest player. However, great players are drawn to a great Coach. They will play hard for a Coach that cares about them, who empowers them, and who challenges them to win.

Never Go Alone

Never do ministry alone. Always take someone with you. Whenever you have a hospital visit to make, first think to yourself who you could invite to drive with you. There have been ministry events I have been invited to speak at where I challenged myself that I would not attend alone. I would call men in my church, or couples in my church until I got one that was available to come along with me.

This sounds like a lot of extra bother, as you may have to adjust your schedule to theirs. You also have to entertain them and make accommodations. But here is the benefit that you are missing: when you bring someone along with you, you are investing in them to teach them how you do what you do. More is caught than taught. You are building relationship with your high-potential people when you spend time with them. And because your time is precious, you are doing ministry AND you are investing in to great people at the same time. When I am traveling to the event, I use the car ride to explain to them what I am getting ready to do, and what they can expect. When I get to the event, I do my ministry and have them watch. Sometimes, if I feel the person is ready, I may even have them help me, by having them pray, or by including them in the care for a person we are there to minister to. Then, on the way back, I ask questions to get them analyzing why I did what I did. By bringing this friend along with me on the journey, I train them, I deepen the relationship, and I have inspired them in their calling to become a minister within our church.

Whenever you have a task to do, stop and ask "who else can do this for me?" If you do not have anyone that you have yet developed, then ask the question "who else can do this with me?" You will need to start with taking people with you and exposing them to ministry. But your mindset is to work from playing basketball

People tend to support what they have helped to create.

on the court to moving to the sidelines. Let the players play. You coach the players. When you allow the players to play the game, which is to do the ministry of the church, they will be much more engaged in the church. People tend to support what they have helped to create. Do you want your people to stop being critical or apathetic standing on the sidelines in your church? Do you want them energized and invested in your church? Put them in the game. Put the ball in their hands. Move from doing to empowering. You will see people become much more engaged in your church.

Recruiting to Build Teams

As a pastor, you likely by now understand that you need volunteers and teams. But I want to teach you how I effectively build teams. I want to shoot down what I see are common practices in churches that do not work well. Be sure you do not put all of your energy in to these practices, only to end up with very few people, or even worse, the wrong people who are not the right fit for your team.

Announcements

Your appeal for people to serve can be ignored and side-stepped from the platform. I have heard the greatest communicators plead with people to serve, and have only a few to no people enlist the next week. While you should let the need be known publicly, understand that your appeal from the platform is not enough to get people to sign on the dotted line.

Sign ups

Sign up tables may bring a few people to your team. But you may not get the right people that you are needing to make your team great. Sure, you may get lucky and have some great person come to your sign up table who has high initiative. But sometimes the people who sign up are people that have not a found a fit anywhere else. They mean well, but they have not developed a skill or a life focus, and they are just wanting to belong. For your team, you don't want people who just want to belong, you want people can help you win.

Undefined Role

Another mistake pastors make is that their ask for help is too general. Just saying that you need help and asking them to show up is not inspiring. People are busy and are not quick to give up their most precious commodity, which is their time. Great people want to know what they are going to be doing, why it is important, and what it looks like specifically. High Capacity people measure everything they do based on results and impact. You need to show them how the part they play will have specific and positive impact for reaching the mission of the church. If you cannot explain in one sentence clearly what their role is and how it is having impact, you are not ready to build your winning team.

Pastors need to take much time to craft the role, the mission, and the measured impact you hope to achieve. You need to define the teams you need, the job description for each person and the serving times that are needed. You may need process-oriented people to help you work through this arduous process. To build teams, you need a team. I have needed help with this, and you will too!

The Power of the Invitation

Personal invitation is the best way to scout out the best players you want. To do this effectively, you must have practiced the first step in my Simple Strategy of loving people well. Here is where the strategy connects from the first step to the second step. And here is where you will begin to see great results! Listen up and pay attention. If you learn this skill and harness it, you will go farther faster. Building a great team will be easy for you and your church will take off like a rocket!

I keep using the word "Scout." I have used the Sports arena where scouts are searching out the potential talent to build their team from. I also think of a Scout as one who hunts. To find the right people, the best talent, you have to start hunting.

Think of a big Lion out on the African Sudan at dusk...hunting time. The Lion is hungry. She has cubs to feed. The Lion is large and ferocious. Her growl can peal the stripes off of a Zebra, and can make the trees shake. Yet, when the Lion is hunting, She grows very still, she remains very quiet. Her stare is fixed on her prey. She watches from afar, hiding in the tall grass so as not to bring attention of her prey standing off in the distance. She edges ever so close to her prey and until suddenly, she makes her move. She chases and pursues her prey! You may thinking...this is how you build teams, Matt? Pretty rough. Ha! I know. Pretty intense.

But, in the same way, with the same focus and intensity, you need to become a great hunter. You need to take time in church to watch, to observe people. Watch from a distance, and don't let them see you. Why? Because people are on their best behavior when the pastor is watching. Let me help you understand something: sometimes the people that pursue you are not the people you want. If they are trying to sell themselves to you, you must ask why. Why do they need this ministry position so bad? And why are they are not serving somewhere else? If they are so gifted, why then are they appealing to you to let them serve? Now, let me back up here and say that EVERY PERSON is valuable. In your church, you should have a place where everyone can belong. But we are talking about building a team, a winning team. Winning teams have winners. I am teaching you how to acquire winners.

Just like the Lion, you need to pursue people. You need to approach people that you have invested in, who you have loved and know well, and ask them to step up and serve. Remember the first step, if done well, earns you the influence to ask them to serve. You will find that they will join your team. They will do it not as much because the vision is so great, but because you personally asked them to.

Have you ever had to move from one house to another? If you have, you know it is a big project. Moving furniture from upstairs to downstairs and then to a moving truck is not my idea of fun. Neither is it to anyone else. I learned the hard way on how building a team works by my first move.

I had asked friends and family to help me, just a few days before moving day. I remember on Saturday morning, only my wife, my father-in-law and my brother-in-law showed. When the first hour had past, they were all frustrated with me asking where all of my friends were. I had asked some friends that I was not as close to. What I learned was that the people that are closest to you are the most committed to you. My family was going to help me move and stay until the end. They would be there whenever I needed. Why? Because they are family. They were not excited about the vision of moving. But they were bought in to me.

The next time I moved, I invited twice as many people to help me as I knew I needed, talking to 15 people not including my family. I also clarified that I needed them for just two hours and then they could leave. I went to people I had built a great relationship with and I approached them three weeks early. I told them that when they would come early, we would start on time and be ready. This time, I had 10 friends show up and the job took less time than planned!

But the real reason these people came out was that I was maturing in my leadership as a pastor. I was investing in their lives well. When I approached them, they responded with "when do you need me? I will be there!" Even before I had told them early Saturday morning, they were already in!

Every Ministry has a Team

Going along with the concept of leaving every conversation "empty-handed", I suggest that for every ministry you have, you need to a build a team around it. Pastor Rich Guerra, who I served under when I was a Music Pastor years ago, heard that I was

You should not be doing ministry. You should be directing ministry.

decorating the stage for a Seasonal Musical I was leading. I was complaining to him that I was sick and overwhelmed after the event. He coached me by saying, "if it takes you to do it, then we should not be doing it." That is good counsel for pastors. You need to change how you think of ministry. Pastor Rich then asked me "how many leaders did you have helping you with the musical, Matt?" He already knew the answer – none. I know your tendency and your pressure is to do ministry and make it happen. But you need to move to the sidelines and get in to the team-building business.

Campaign

When building a ministry team, use the concept of launching a campaign. You need to create energy around the ministry. When scouting out great people, share the need with them and bring them in to the conversation. I find that most leaders attempt to recruit people with the need all figured out, with the problem solved. All they want are people that will do the work. This is another reason why you may be struggling with getting high capacity people. You will find that people want to be included early in the process. They need see the problem and sense the urgency to solve the problem. A great campaign is all about exposing a problem and rallying people to get involved in finding the solution. That is your job.

Pastor Todd Mullins, my pastor at Christ Fellowship is great at building teams. Our church excels at building what we call the Dream Team. Pastor Todd taught me that when I approach people, bring my ideas "half-baked." Bring your ideas not fully processed. Leave some of the obstacles unsolved. Come with great questions, and then let people bring answers to them. What does this do? It allows people to step up to the challenge and be the hero. While Pastor Todd has already worked through his objectives and processes, he holds back sharing all that is in his mind with the people he is enlisting. Rather, he engages them in the process and invites them along on the journey of discovery. This is great leadership!

One of the best ways to attract highly gifted, high capacity people to your team is to engage them in to the conversation of the ministry. While you cannot just let everyone do what they want, you can create room in the conversation for others to give input. You as the leader need to keep the conversation flowing toward the best idea and keep your mission front and center. But your goal with every ministry, every facet of your church's operations must have a team built around it to own it, to look after it.

Pastors – build teams around you. Hand them the ball, and give them permission to play the game. Help them win, supporting them with great coaching. They will enjoy serving in the church and, as a result, they will be more connected TO the church.

Triple Threat Process #3:

Develop Leaders

 The third step in the Triple Threat Process is to focus on developing leaders from the teams you have built. Notice that I do not try to first recruit leaders so that I can build the teams. I do not try to find leaders first before I start loving all people well. If you are a systematic-minded person, you may disagree with me. You may see on your flow chart that you need some captains listed at the top so you can build down your structure from there. But I have learned that in order to find the right leaders, and the ready leaders, I must focus on this step last. Here is why.

If I have loved people well, and if I have taken the time to build trust and relationship with them, I have now earned permission to invite them to join my team. As the pastor, you know the myriad of needs that each need a ministry built to meet those needs. You know the many teams it takes to accomplish all of the ministries. With so many people serving on so many teams, you will not be able to lead them all well. You are only one person, and you cannot give every area of the church the attention it deserves. You need leaders. And you need them badly.

Leaders are not born. I do not believe there is such a thing as a "natural born leader." I may be wrong. Certainly, there are personality types that naturally attract people to them. Of course, it does not hurt to be good looking. Talent always helps. Some of the best leaders were not the obvious choice to people. David in the Bible was the last pick. Winston Churchill was elected only after a national crisis. Whether a person has naturally strong qualities, or possesses hidden depth, all leaders must be developed. Their skills and wisdom must be forged in the fire. And it takes a long time going through a process for people to get it.

Most pastors find themselves desperate for capable leaders now. Like, immediately. Pastors have vision, and they need gifted people to step up and lead. Pastors tend to look outside their church to find experienced people to come in and take leadership. But most pastors cannot afford expensive All Star leaders to bring to their church. Or if they can afford high-priced stars, they many times find they are disappointed when the leader proves ineffective at creating results. Other times, the outside leader has his own agenda and can even draw the people within church to their personal agenda and vision!

Do you know where the best leaders can be found? Do you know where your greatest effectiveness and church growth can come from? Right under your nose. Yes – they are in your very midst right now. You don't see them, you tell me? Let me show you how to see them. Come closer. Take a look and let me show you what I see. Learn to see the rough piece of coal that can become a diamond. I love the analogy that Pastor Julie Mullins uses in looking for the potential in our people. She says that when she is looking at our people at Christ Fellowship church, she is mining for gold. She is digging and drudging. She is searching. And she believes that every person has gold in them. But it takes someone to work to dig, to search. The pastor must use his magnifying glass to look for the gold potential.

I believe your best leaders come from within your church. Your best leaders are with you at this very moment. Sure, they may not be nearly ready. They do not see it in themselves yet. Your best leaders are not staff members. They may not have graduated from Seminary or Bible School. But there are people right now in your church family who love God and love to be used of

God. They serve faithfully and with pure motive. There are some people who are a part of your team that remain steady, who solve problems, who do not give up.

The advantage of developing leaders who are in your church is massive. When you think you must draft leaders from another church, or another place, you have many disadvantages. They will not know your heart. People coming from outside your church family have not yet internalized the vision and mission of your church. They will have to move and will not know the region or the culture. You will always be guessing their agenda. Are they just looking for a career move? Are they running away from problems thinking the grass is greener with you? When you develop leaders who are with you now, all of these cautions become non-issues. These people live in the area of your church. They are already bought in to the mission and heart of the church. They have no agenda because they already serve. They are not looking for promotion or position because they have already established their life and career. THESE are the people you want to begin to pour your life into. THESE are the people that you are to begin developing.

Get Out of the Way

To take on the mindset of developing leaders, you will be forced you to change your focus – big time. You see, you probably think that you can keep leading the church, leading all of the ministries and caring for all of the people, and then tack on this little step. That's not how this works, and it won't work if you just tack this on.

> Shift your focus from doing to developing.

This mindset shift must take place in order for to realize: you cannot lead alone. You cannot be the only leader, the only pastor. To develop leaders, you will need to change your work schedule rhythm, change how you make decisions for the church, change how you make the ministries happen. No longer will you be the central figure. No longer will every idea, every initiative come from only you. You will need to shift your focus from doing to developing.

A big part of developing people is to simply get out of their way. It may not make sense to you, but your leadership may be blocking them from growing and developing. When you get out of their way, you MAKE A WAY for them to begin their leadership journey.

When you think of developing leaders, your logical instinct will be to have a training class where you teach leadership 101. You may love to create visual presentations and hand-outs with the purpose of teaching people how you do what you do. You may even go one step farther by setting up monthly meetings for you to do some in-depth training with them. Are these bad to do? Probably not. They have their place.

But I have learned from experience that all the training and teaching in the world a leader does not make. Some of the most well-meaning people who have been to leadership conferences, who read books and who have been invested in never actually materialize in to great leaders. They love the training and appreciate the investment. But some people are more in love with learning than leading. Why? Because leadership is hard. Many start down the path of leading people, but they did not do the necessary work required to grow their capacity. They found that no one would actually follow them. No one would change their life because of their leadership. It is like watching work out videos hoping you will lose weight. It does not work that way. It takes work. It requires personal growth.

Watch Them Grow

How do you develop a team member in to a leader? And what makes a truly great leader?

In the next chapter, I am going to show you how to look for and raise up the right kind of people. But, in this third step in my process to be a Strategic Pastor, I want to give some insights and tools in how I develop these potential people for greatness in your church.

Highlight their strengths, cover their weaknesses

The most important principle in developing a follower in to a leader is to show them what you see – their potential. Their gift. This reaches back to Julie Mullin's concept to mine for gold. It amazes me how we all tend to focus on our weaknesses and not our strengths. Why is this? Because we feel everyone is looking at our weaknesses and criticizing. The truth is, we are our worst critic. Because we are fragile and emotional, we tend to live in fear and shame of our mistakes. And when we see others shine where we struggle, it shrinks us down to feeling like we have nothing to give.

As the pastor, you are to draw out people's gifts. Bring attention to their gifts, first to them, and then to others. And don't be surprised if it takes them some time to recognize it for themselves.

A young man in my church was raising a family and was active in our church. He and his wife would serve when asked and led a home group with young couples. I first noticed a gift in Travis O'Neal when I had a men's gathering in a home to watch a basketball game. I had invited many new, younger men to the event with the intent of getting them connected. The room felt a bit awkward and most of the guys were just sitting watching the game quietly. When Travis walked through the door, the men came alive. Travis was loud, happy, and fun. He had Mountain Dew in one hand, and potato chips in the other. He had a baseball cap on his head and was wearing athletic gear. Before Travis entered the scene, the group the environment was dull and boring. As soon as he arrived, the mood changed entirely. Travis already knew a few of the guys, but he began connecting with those he didn't.

I remember the next week inviting Travis to lunch. I saw raw potential and wanted to invest time in to him. As we drove to the restaurant, I relived the scene with him. As Travis listened to my telling the story again, he laughed and just made fun of himself. I told him that he had a gift with people. He dismissed it, but I had planted a seed in his mind. I told him that his gift was powerful and that he could grow one day in to a person who influences others.

As I started utilizing Travis within the church, in speaking in front of people, he would be very nervous. He always told me that he would much rather I do the speaking, and he would be content with assisting me. I knew the areas he was weak in with speaking. I could see he still thought like a team member. Travis spent enough time with me to see the work and discipline it takes to be a pastor.

What I did with Travis was continually feature his strengths with people, while covering over the areas that I knew were not yet developed. I was slow to correct, quick to celebrate. *Pay attention at this point in the story: people need much more celebration than they do correction.* I know you may see the misses, the wrong attitudes, the blind spots. But ignore a lot of that, and cover over it in the beginning. Rather, bring attention to their passion, their drive, and feature their natural strengths.

I kept painting a picture for Travis of more. He saw himself as a man who served in church. I wanted to show him that he could be a leader in the church. I talked him in to taking a couple of staff roles at different times, while still working a full time job. This was scary for him, because he was having to learn leadership quickly, and I needed him to produce. What Travis did intuitively was to use who he was and how he was made to get people to follow him. I remember him saying to me he did not think he was leading correctly. But the definition of a leader is that others are following. People were beginning to follow him. And people were growing spiritually because of him.

Travis loved Coach Tom Mullins because Travis was an athlete and responded to his style of leadership. I told Travis that he had that same anointing that Pastor Tom had. I encouraged Travis to use some of the same techniques that Coach used. *Stop the story here: when you paint a picture and point to a person for your developing leader, it helps them see what they can become. As people, **we develop***

> **As people, we develop more by how we emulate then how we educate.**

more by how we emulate then how we educate.

Travis developed his leadership, growing himself in our church. I had the privilege to watch him grow. I simply got out of his way, gave him the gift of time, and kept pointing out his gifts and strengths, both to him, and to everyone around him. Today, Travis O'Neal leads the most exciting Christ Fellowship Campus, with many people's lives being transformed by the power of Jesus. Travis is a gifted, passionate and effective pastor. He has worked hard to continue to sharpen himself. God is using Travis in ways he never thought possible.

Conclusion

The most significant piece to the Triple Threat Process of a Pastor is this: Developing the potential in the people God has given you will bring the greatest joy and give you the biggest impact in your ministry. When you take the time to develop the calling in someone else, it will expand your calling. You will go farther faster. You will reach through others. Embrace the pastoral call of the Apostle Paul and develop leaders. You will move from the math of addition to the miracle of multiplication.

I have dedicated the next chapter to continue the discussion of developing leaders. I want to give some specifics on how to identify the right people, how to recruit them and then empower them.

Chapter 4   Triple Threat Process for Strategic Pastors

Study Questions

The first step in the Triple Threat Process is to Love People. When it comes to knowing people, what have you found is the most difficult part of getting to know them? What takes the most time? What are some of the barriers to building relationship with people for you? Why?

The second step is to Build Teams. If you struggle to build teams around you, what can you pinpoint are your fears and excuses? List those out and create an assignment of what you are going do to get better. If you are a natural team builder, what do you do well that you must pass on to others? If you are playing the "addition game" in building team, how are going to train others to build team so you can move to the "multiplication game?"

The third step is to Develop Leaders. Do an evaluation test on yourself in your ability to see leadership in people. Do you tend to be a doer or a developer? Do you see the potential in people for more, or do you struggle with that? Who is a great developer that you know who you can begin working closely with? That is the only way you will push yourself to grow as a developer.

Chapter 5

Identifying Potential Leaders

Similar to previous sections, I want to first address some of the tendencies I see in pastors when they think of developing leaders. Below are common mistakes that we all make inadvertently when trying to work with leaders.

The Limited Leader

Pastors will recruit a person to be a leader in their church, but limit their ability to lead. This is unintentional, for sure by the pastor, because the whole reason the pastor has called this person to lead is to take some responsibility for an aspect of the church. However, the pastor continues to be in all of the decision conversations. The pastor is always solving the problems of the leader. The pastor must approve purchases and wants to sign off on details. Therefore, the leader becomes very limited in their scope and ability to make an impact in their area.

The limited leader will end up managing just the small, day to day operations, and will actually play more the role of a task-oriented worker, not a leader. Or, if the leader has vision and capacity for more, the leader will quickly resign from the role and go somewhere else where he can have more room to influence and lead. When the pastor limits leaders, he is still leading the team, and his limited leader simply becomes another person he must think for.

The Silent Leader

Pastors will raise up a leader to lead people, but will never give the leader a chance to speak, teach, or communicate. This is due to the fact that most of us as pastors love to speak, love to preach, love to communicate. In fact, if we were honest, one of the big draws for you being a pastor is that you thought you were going to preach! You were going to teach people like Jesus did. Many pastors think that if they could delegate all other responsibilities, they could then just get to preach and teach.

A pastor should be the primary communicator for sure. People look to the pastor to teach God's Word and to bring spiritual leadership to the church family. Therefore, He should clearly be focusing on preaching and teaching. But if you are always the person who leads in prayer, who leads every meeting, who leads every teaching or devotional thought, you are drawing people to your leadership only. The key word here is ONLY. People will never buy in to other leaders if you do not let them hear other voices.

The Apprehensive Leader

Are your leaders apprehensive to make a decision? Are they slow to step out? When is the last time they did something fresh or creative? Are they just doing the same program with the same few people? If the answer is yes to any of these questions, you may have not given clear role descriptions for your leaders. They are unsure of where your leadership ends and their leadership begins. No clear lines have been defined, so they will not overstep some else's authority space.

Another cause of this symptom is when the pastor is second guessing decisions, making last minute changes, or correcting leaders often. People have a fear of failure and want to please. When they are having to look over their shoulder for a possible change or correction, the last thing they will do is try something bold or risky. And yet, boldness, risk and creativity is what the church desperately needs in order to be effective.

The Under Challenged Leader

Sure, every person on your team should be willing to serve where needed. Nothing should be beneath a true Servant Leader. However, your leaders may be unchallenged. How can you tell? They are missing Sundays. They are slow to respond to communication. If you had a great leader, you will not enjoy having them for long. Why? They are now in another church, or not in church at all. Why is that? You may have loved them and cared for them well. Why would they still be pulling away?

It is not that they do not feel loved and appreciated. It is not that the work is too hard. On the contrary, it is not challenging them. There is no obstacle to overcome for their leadership. There is no pressing, urgent need that they can solve. Great leaders want to be the hero, they want to have great impact. High capacity people want to win the game. They need competition, they need purpose. Have you not shared a vision that is so compelling, so stretching, so exciting? Then you may have some under challenged leaders... and you will not keep them around for long.

Identifying Leaders

Ok, now for the good stuff. How do you recruit leaders?

Well, you need to back up and ask some good questions before recruiting leaders:

What makes a good leader?

Where do you find them? How?

How do you get good leaders to agree to lead?

These are better questions to start with. I first want to give you my definition of what constitutes a leader. A leader is a person that others are following. That's it. I did not mention leadership skills. I did not mention tall, dark and handsome. I did not consider their outgoing personality, or ability to share vision. From my perspective, if I see that someone, anyone is following a person in some way, that is the litmus test that a leader demonstrates an ability to lead people.

A great place to look in judging leadership is to start in the home. Is the person influencing their marriage well? Either a man or a woman can do this, even if the man is the Spiritual Leader. Is the parent influencing their children in a way that they are responsive and follow? No family is perfect, but if there is harmony, purpose and health in the home, this is a great indicator for a potential leader. That is why the Apostle Paul states the requirement of a pastor is to first lead well in the home.

In this simple strategy of loving people, building teams, and developing leaders, I want to show you that your potential leaders are probably already in front of you. They are likely serving faithfully on one of your teams. Is every team member a potential leader? No. But, looking at the great people on your teams will help you identify your next leaders. I have a 3 step process I use to identify leaders from my teams.

Observe

Test

Empower

Observe

How do you recruit leaders, you ask? How do you know how to identify the right kind of people? You have to create space to stop and watch. Go bird watching. On Sundays, you need to take yourself out of a leadership role sometimes and hide in the back and just watch. And when you are walking through your church, notice how your team operates. When people approach you, you are evaluating them. What are you looking for? What qualities? While you may need different types of leaders for different positions and ministry needs, I want to touch on a few common traits to be on the look-out for:

Attractional

People who always have a crowd around them are attractional. And the amazing thing to me is that many times, these attractional people do not even realize that they have this gift. I have had to show people that they have the gift to draw people to them. I remember a Student Leader who worked with me had this amazing gift. Brandon Marlow would place himself out in the courtyard in between church services, and there would always be a crowd surrounding him. Not only would students be with him, but parents and even adults. It was amazing how he could draw a crowd with his great personality and ability to make people feel special. While all leaders may not be highly extroverted, they do need to show you that they can draw people. And be careful to notice if they are going to people, or if people are drawn to them. I have met some driven, dominant personalities who desire to lead and will bombard people. However, no one is following them, they are just enduring them.

Wise

Some leaders may not draw huge crowds to them, but you will find some who have a tightly knit group of friends and people they are connected with. One trait to listen for is for people who demonstrate maturity and wisdom. They are slow to speak, and do not take the spotlight. But you constantly notice discernment, good judgement and witness their steadiness and consistency.

This trait has proven essential to have on my team close to me. A gifted young lady, Talena Howard led alongside me for many years, and helping me navigate tough decisions, adapting to change, and leveraging few resources we had to make a lot out of them. People followed Talena because she had a steadiness about her and brought measured discernment. People around her appreciated her leadership because of her wisdom.

Resourceful

People who look for ways to win, who are innovative and find creative solutions will draw talent and will compel people to come work for them. Look for ingenuity, and for people who prove resourceful. A young man named Adam Baldwin approached me offering creative solutions to a rented garage we were using for a Student space for our young, portable church. He scavenged and searched for materials while at the same time enlisting family and friends to help him create his design. He quickly became indispensable to me with these gifts he brought to the table. As he led events and projects on our team, he always asked two questions: 1. What if? 2. Who Else? People followed Adam because he was always pursuing excellence in an exciting way. He learned how to harness the greatness in people by producing his dream through people.

Empowering

The Leader that empowers people will garner great loyalty from those people. To empower people means one must interact well with people and learn how they are wired. I noticed Michelle Morehouse had potential gifting for church leadership in my first conversation with her. When I threw her in to ministry on our Stuart Campus team, she assessed all aspects of her responsibilities and then quickly looked for capable people within the church that she could empower to fulfill those tasks. Sometimes, she would ask me if I was alright with her delegating as much as she did. I was all for it! In fact, the more that she empowered people to do the ministry, the more leadership I would entrust to her. Michelle enjoys helping people think like leaders, not like followers. She encourages, challenges, and asks great questions of her leaders, which stretch them. Michelle is so great at developing people around her so that they are empowered to lead within the church. And her people love her for it!

While qualities of talent, of faithfulness, of attitude are important, I am focusing you to look for these specific qualities when scouting for a leader. Because I define a leader as someone who others are following, attraction, wisdom, resourcefulness and caring are the top traits that people will follow.

Test

The next step in Identifying leaders is to begin testing people. When you look at the teams you have built, you have already put them through a test of sorts. You have observed the "unteachables" that Leadership Expert David Anderson talks about. He suggests that while there are many skills you can teach, there are some attributes that cannot be taught:

- **Character**
- **Drive**
- **Energy**
- **Passion**
- **Talent**
- **Attitude**

In testing future leaders, the Bible gives us great wisdom in how to properly do this:

Luke 16:10
"If you are faithful in little things, you will be faithful in large ones. But if you are dishonest in little things, you won't be honest with greater responsibilities. 11 And if you are untrustworthy about worldly wealth, who will trust you with the true riches of heaven? 12 And if you are not faithful with other people's things, why should you be trusted with things of your own?

This verse is so rich with insight. That last part teaches us that leadership of more should always be handled with keeping in mind that it is not ours to do with as we choose. Leadership means responsibility.

The way to test people is with small responsibilities at first. I have learned the hard way that it is not wise to take a great team member and immediately appoint them the leader. You need to give leadership gradually and incrementally. Rather than hand them the whole team and the entire responsibility at once, give them small, one time opportunities to FEEL leadership before they TAKE ON leadership.

When our Stuart Campus needed a Live Production Coordinator, I saw a man apply for the position named Dan Burd. While he had the qualifications for the role, I noticed that Dan also had theatre background, with a gift of creativity. I took particular interest in these auxiliary gifts, as our church had just finished a creative outreach idea called At the Movies. For this outreach, our Campus transforms in to a movie set, with the teaching series themed from blockbuster movies. At the Movies proved to be a great draw to unchurched people to try church. Yet, our Campus did not present At the Movies well the year before. Our team currently did not have a strong Creative, nor a set designer.

The next year, I enlisted Dan to help our team with the creative aspects of At the Movies. Because I felt the ultimate responsibility for the project of our Campus, I took charge, with Dan using his gifts. This first time around, I wanted to test Dan's ability and capacity. I watched Dan speak in to the project, and I observed how he interacted with volunteers. How much would he DO? How much would he EMPOWER? How hard would he work? How committed would he be when things got difficult?

Dan showed not only his gifts, but also showed his ability to work well with people. He proved he could work hard. Dan proved that he could help take an idea to completion and implementation. That year, At the Movies was so great, that our Campus received an award from Leadership! The next year, I empowered Dan Burd to officially lead our At the Movies project, with me focusing on other aspects of the Campus. The next year, we won an award again!

Stretch

Your testing opportunities need to stretch people. I believe you test them in areas of strengths AND of weakness. Why? So they can be more aware of where they will flourish and where they desperately need support. The other reason to test them in many areas is that sometimes what they think is their weakness actually is not. It may be that they have not developed the muscles in a needed skill.

When Pastor Todd was developing me as a Campus Pastor, he coached me on leading altar calls at the end of his message. I had not had any training previously on public speaking, having been a musician previously. My first altar calls had no one coming forward. I made excuses blaming it on the room, the screen, and not having enough time to talk. Pastor Todd kept coaching me and pushing me to work on this skill and stretch myself. I remember when I first had a few people come forward, I realized that I actually COULD lead this spiritual moment. This happened only after months of watching the masters, practicing and improving. I am so glad I was stretched to try an area that I was weak in. As a result, I learned a new skill that has served me well in becoming a better pastor.

Risk

Testing your people means you have to take a risk. That's right. Your person may fail. News flash, pastor: they WILL fail. And when the person you are developing fails, it means the ministry may fail. For you, that likely means that you will have some damage control on your hands. But the greatest lessons are learned through failure. Why? Because when people fail, they are paying great attention to why they failed. That means they are focused specifically on what went wrong.

My friend and boss, Bill Tumulty is a great developer of leaders. He has helped me grow tremendously and has skills that differ from my own, which add tools to my leadership I previously did not possess. He has told me how he will stand and watch developing leaders at a major church event like Easter and witness them fail at leading. While others want to go in and save the day, he will give space and allow them to fail; or rather, allow them to learn. Bill's philosophy is to let people fail enough so they will self-correct as they continue learning, but to not let them fail so that it endangers their calling or the church's ministry. Testing people means taking some small risks so people can learn and see in real time.

Testing takes time. It takes many tests to allow people to see what leadership looks like and feels like. Testing will take creativity and intentionality on your part. This step is symbiotic with an earlier principle I shared: never do ministry alone. Always take someone with you. You can test people best when you are standing with them, when you are in the room. Testing sometimes means allowing them to run an event, or a meeting, or watching them build a team without you. You have to give them stretch steps and also take risks with them, so you can then measure their gifts, their maturity and their capacity. Testing tells you a lot of where they are at and what they will need from you to grow.

Empower

When you have observed the "unteachables," having tested people in small ways, you will have a few that are ready to rise. I wish I could promise you that you can get many people to this status, but I would be lying. I have invested in and tested many people, but most I have worked with capped at some level and never developed to the level that I could fully empower them. Only a few people were able to climb the cliffs of the leadership mountain to a point that I could begin empowering them with leadership of the church. But the few that made the climb were worth the investment.

One way I test people who come to me with ambition to lead is to give them a leadership challenge. This goes back to leaving every interaction with people empty-handed, so that I give them clear steps to take. If they want my time investment, they must have completed the challenge first. As the pastor, I have so many who want my time and attention, but I only invest more in to those that were diligent to do the hard work it takes to become a leader.

One such man was John Chitty. I saw his passion for God and for people. The way I met John was when I was looking for people to help me tear down chairs after church in a school cafeteria. I asked a group of people who were in the front row to help me, and they all agreed. John and his wife Lisa were part of the lucky group I enlisted. Every week, John kept coming back to serve. So I started spending time with him. He shared with me how God had helped him personally and had helped strengthen his marriage. I challenged John to go find men in our church and invest in them. (I say this to people who want me to mentor them: "go find 7 people and start a group with them.") John went and did this. He began meeting with men and caring for them. He went above and beyond. While John was in a group himself, he also led another men's group. Consequently, I continued giving John more leadership. John became one of the greatest mentors to men our Stuart Campus has to this day. Marriages have been saved. Men who were apathetic are now passionate for God. John's phone blows up with texts from his men. John is a powerful leader who I have empowered to lead people in our church, much like a pastor on staff.

Another couple similar to John and Lisa Chitty who I connected with in our church were Tom and Kellie Agulia. They showed passion and commitment, and were gifted with skill and insight to see opportunity for ministry. I needed their gifts to help me see opportunities in our community for our church to go out and serve. Tom and Kellie were creative, tenacious and were great builders of partnerships that helped to connect Christ Fellowship to many organizations. I soon learned that I could empower them to create the event, lead the charge, and assemble large amounts of volunteers to accomplish the vision. Their pioneering of Saturday projects and seasonal outreaches helped form what Christ Fellowship now calls Fourth Saturday Serve.

Empowering Leaders means that you create space for them to lead. Pastor Todd says "Great leaders create space for others to lead." I love that. This reminds me when I used to teach piano lessons years ago. I would struggle to get the students to perform the songs I was teaching them. I had a parent make a suggestion to me that maybe I should not try to teach the song by playing it. Rather, I should have the student sit at the piano and teach them as they try to play it. After I thought about this suggestion, I realized the wisdom in this. The student would never learn to play the song if my hands were playing the piano more than they were. For the student to learn the song, I would have to take my hands off the keys. To empower great leaders, you must take your hands off.

Leaders Who Rise Around You

As our church and ministries grew, I knew I needed more leaders and more gifted leaders. But how would I handle having a leader that was effective as I was at leading? What if I realize that some of the people leading under me actually have better skills than I do? What do I do with that? How would you handle that?

I started as Campus Pastor at Christ Fellowship at 34 years old. I had the energy and youth to stay relevant to reaching young families. However, as I moved in to my forties, I realized I would not effectively reach people in their twenties. I also discovered that my leadership language and my approach to church ministry was more conventional, and culture was evolving. How would I stay effective and relevant to lead our church? I prayed for a leader who was high capacity and who would complement my gifts and life season.

Our Student Pastor was DJ Cabrera. When he joined the team, I noticed his character, his desire to be effective, and his ability to lead himself well. He worked hard to figure out a way to grow our Student ministry, which met in a small room in the rented high school. He grew the Student ministry to more than double, and had built a strong culture of empowering young leaders under him. When our Campus went through transition with some staff being promoted to other positions, I realized that the leader I was praying for was sitting right in front of me. DJ was becoming that leader for our Stuart Campus.

I began empowering DJ to lead in higher leadership opportunities. I invited him to help me make decisions. I also invited him to speak in to areas that were beyond his direct responsibility. I noticed his gift of communicating and began sharing the platform with him. DJ was already great when he had joined the team. But I believe when I allowed him to rise around me as a prominent voice in our church, he began learning new skills and building unused muscles he never thought he had.

Allowing DJ to rise with me as a leader not only developed his calling and gifts, it benefited our Stuart Campus. Today, we have become a dynamic duo, with me reaching my generation and DJ reaching his younger generation. Rather than seen as having competing leadership, we enjoy a complementing leadership. Our Stuart Campus at Christ Fellowship has moved from adding people to multiplying people and is healthier than ever.

When you allow high capacity people to rise around you, it produces many benefits, with no down side.

Margin

Pastor, what you need in order to incorporate all of the principles in Strategic Pastor is MARGIN. How else can you have the time or focus to begin implementing these strategies? The biggest benefit I appreciated was that by empowering a great person to rise with me allowed me more space to prepare, to evaluate, and to invest. The more DJ would be seen by others as a prominent leader, the more I did not have to keep my hand on the steering wheel. Who is the one high capacity person you trust and believe in to take a prominent role in your church? They are the answer to creating the much needed margin you need to begin to lead like a Strategic Pastor.

What people want the most from their Pastor is their time.

Multiplier

Your church has so many needs, so much vision, so many ministry opportunities, that there is enough leadership for both you and the leader who leads alongside you. Believe me. If you have to be the face of the place, that means you will have to lead everything. What would it be like if the two of you split up some of the initiatives and responsibilities? That would mean you both could give more focus, more creativity, more leadership to make it grow! Letting a great leader rise around you multiplies your reach.

Touch

Answer this question: what would you say is the number one thing people want from their Lead Pastor? Bible teaching? Vision? Success? Wrong. I think it is their time.

People want to know their pastor. And they want their pastor to know them. This reaches back to the foundational step one of Strategic Pastor: Love People.

If you have another prominent leader who you have empowered to rise with you, guess what? More people will feel known and loved by their pastor. Earlier in the book, I mentioned that you should not try to know everyone. But everyone wants to be known by their pastor. You will need to get comfortable with the realization that some people may love him more than you. Learn to accept that and understand that this is a big benefit to you and helps the church feel like a family.

The other benefit I learned of having trusted leaders lead the platform on Sunday was that I could now walk the halls, walk outside, and connect with people. I was able to meet people, recruit team members, and observe potential leaders, all without worrying about leading from the platform. The response I got from people was remarkable. They loved getting time with me. Some of these people I would follow up with for care, some for connecting them to the church, and some for investing more in them. I had done more in one Sunday to help shepherd and build our church than I could have done in three months!

Learn the benefit of allowing deserving leaders to rise around you. Don't hold them down. Lift them up. Only you can do this for people. They cannot do it on their own. They would never try to overshadow you. But the greatest talent have the greatest dreams. They need to be challenged, and they need the opportunity to reach their full potential. If you are willing to share your leadership with others, yours will not be diminished. It will expand. Your church will reach farther than you ever thought possible.

Leaders Who Reach Beyond You

Ok, I may have you a bit nervous now. You may feel like I am taking away your leadership. How far are you taking this, Matt? What about me? Well, I will show you.

Yes, it is possible that some leaders will even become more prominent than you. In fact, if you were honest, you would admit that you are not the greatest leader there ever was. Don't worry – I am not the greatest leader in my church. I know that, because I am surrounded by geniuses. I cannot take credit for any success I have experienced at Christ Fellowship. I have been privileged to receive encouragement, mentoring, opportunity and resources. The truth is, most people would find success in serving at Christ Fellowship. It is a great church that cultivates a healthy culture. Healthy things grow in rich soil.

What does it look like to actually allow leaders who have more capacity and more gift to rise beyond you? If you look at your journey as a story, and less like a competition, you begin to think about your legacy. When you begin to celebrate the people in your life more than the successes in your life, then you will get excited about those who shine brighter than you.

Many of the people I have mentioned in this book are leaders who have achieved great success, moving beyond my church and leading in greater ways. I am so proud of them, and I stay in contact with all of them.

One of the leaders I am most excited about is my very own daughter, Madison. She looks a lot like me and she shares my personality and passions. At an early age, I noticed she took to music when I sat her down on the piano bench to test her. As she grew, I saw the same gifts that I have for music and with people emerge in her. Through teaching and development opportunities I have given her, she is way ahead of where I was when I was her age as a teenager. Part of that is Christ Fellowship is a great place for any budding talent to develop and experience large scale ministry. She has led worship in front of large crowds, teaches piano students as her job, and is already half way through with earning her BSN degree in Nursing. People tell my wife, Kellie and I how impressed they are with our beautiful daughter. They always think she is older than she is, because she is so accomplished. Can you tell I am proud?

As I have watched Madison develop herself and be featured in one of the greatest churches in America, I am so excited at what God has in store for her. She will reach levels in music and church ministry that will go beyond my capacity. And the great thing is, Madison is so grateful for my love and development of her. When you allow great people to rise beyond you, they will look and point back to you.

Conclusion

The most gratifying thing you will do as a pastor is to help people grow to their God-given potential. And the most exciting people that you will help grow are those who have the potential to lead in your church. When you identify the right people by observing, testing and empowering, you move from the math of addition in your church to multiplication.

In this next chapter, I want to talk to you about building a special group of people that will help you realize your heart and vision for your church.

Chapter 5   Identifying Potential Leaders

Study Questions

In order to identify potential leaders within your church, we must first do the hard work of doing an honest evaluation of our leadership. Our ability to draw greater leaders to us is limited by the health and skill of our own leadership. Which type of leader do you tend to draw listed below? What are you doing to cause this?

The Limited Leader
The Silent Leader
The Apprehensive Leader
The Under Challenged Leader

To identify potential leaders, the first practice is to observe people. Of all of the qualities described, which do you most naturally see first? Which do you need more help seeing in people?

Attractional
Caring
Wisdom
Resourceful

The second practice is to test people. When have you tested people where it has worked? When has it failed? And the bigger question is, did it actually fail? Or did it actually teach them and teach you insights? Explain.

The third practice is to empower people to lead. Describe a time when you stretched a person's skills and capacity too far.

Chapter 6

The Inner Circle

You may already be familiar with the concept of an inner circle. Not all of the concepts I am presenting in Strategic Pastor are new ideas, I know. What am I doing is simply laying out the strategy I have formed that has brought me success in my calling as a pastor. I hope you will learn the wisdom in these principles and will incorporate some of them in areas of your leadership so you can expand your capacity and see more impact.

Presidents have their Cabinet. King Arthur had his Knights of the Round Table. Jesus had His twelve disciples. These are all forms of an inner circle that surround the leader. Or rather, that the leader invites to surround him. Do you have an inner circle?

I first was made aware of needing an inner circle when I was being coached by our Founding Pastor, Dr. Tom Mullins. Pastor Tom would come in to our Campus Pastor meeting once in a while to spend meaningful time with us. Of course, a Coach cannot help but start coaching, and so Pastor Tom began asking us questions, likely to gauge where our level of leadership was. He asked us "who is in your inner circle?" We all sat silently and looked at each other for someone to speak. Pastor Tom then followed with "do any of you have an inner circle?" When the room still remained silent, Pastor Tom began drawing the picture for us.

"Every leader needs a Peter, Paul and John in their lives. Jesus drew them closer to Him more than He did the other disciples. If Jesus did this, so should we." Pastor Tom began naming his key men in the church that he has brought in to his inner circle. He explained how each man had different gifts that bring different value to him. He claimed that these men had been essential in keeping him encouraged, wise, and supported. After Pastor Tom was finished with his coaching, he began going down the row to ask "if you had to pick three people at your Campus that would be your inner circle, who would it be?"

Thankfully, I was fifth in line, so I had time to think. I began to think through who I trusted the most, who I had the most relationship with, and who was the most vital to me leading effectively. When Pastor Tom finally asked me, I responded with my three: Adam, Travis and Talena. I had never thought of them before as my inner circle. At first, it felt a bit scary when I called them that, because I knew their weaknesses and their shortcomings. Could I really trust them to be my inner circle? And then I thought about other staff and other families who I loved and trusted. What would they think? Is that fair to just pick three?

I left that meeting forever changed. My mind had been expanded. My understanding of leadership had been revolutionized. You see, I am the kind of person that when I hear something wise or creative, I must act on it. I have a bias toward action. I want to see positive results. So, I had to begin figuring out how to re-orient my team, my time and my Campus structure to implement an inner circle model. When I did, it revolutionized the Campus and great things started to happen.

Let me coach you the way I was coached. Allow me to put you on the spotlight now, pastor. Who is in your inner circle? Do you even have an inner circle? If the answer is you are not sure, then your answer is really a NO. Don't worry. Many pastors have never taken the time to build an inner circle around them . You may answer "my staff." Others of you may say "my Elder Board." OK. Those may be your inner circle. But too many of you are leading alone. You are carrying all of the spiritual weight and responsibility of the church alone. You may have teams, leaders and staff helping you, but you still feel all alone. Most pastors do. Inner circle will fix that!

Inner Circle Defined

Definition is always helpful, isn't it? We talk about these concepts of leaders, vision, inner circle, but it is vital that we clearly specify what something is, and what purpose it serves. Otherwise, we read something that sounds great, but just move back to what is working for us. What works for you now won't work to get you to the higher call and greater vision God has given you. To reach farther, you must form a trusted band of players close around you. Here is my three-sided definition of inner circle, and the benefits that it gives you as a pastor.

Inner Circle Definition:

People who love you
Partners who support you
Pastors who extend you

Your inner circle people will have different personalities and gifts. Some may come from your staff, other from your Elder Board. Some may just be people within your church that you feel have earned the right to be brought closer. While you may select some who are outside of the church for Inner Circle, I would oppose that notion. My reason is that they need to be in the church so they can better know how to support you. Trusted people outside of your church may serve better as mentors and personal friends. But Inner Circle people ought to be actively a part of your church family.

People Who Love You

You need people who believe in you, who absolutely love you. While a pastor should not try to please people, you ought to have built relationship with people that you love and who love you back. I have people like this who love me and my family.

They care for me and encourage me often. They care for my family and always looking for ways to add value to us. As a pastor, you need to feel that someone cares for you, who is concerned for your personal well- being. Feeling loved and valued by your inner circle will breathe life in to your heart and will keep you encouraged when you have the hard seasons in ministry.

It can be challenging to find people who do this well. What do I mean? Probably everybody in your church loves you, I assume. They all appreciate you. But you need a certain quality person who loves without wanting anything in return. This is harder to accomplish than it sounds. Every person, in truth wants something in return. Even the purest individual needs from you. That is not wrong or selfish; it is just human. But when it comes to choosing people to be in your inner circle, you must gauge the thermometer of how much they NEED from you versus how much capacity they have to LOVE you.

Do not gauge people's love according to how much they do for you. Do not measure their capacity to love based on free meals and gifts. My dad taught me "Matt, there is no such thing as a free lunch." I laugh when I think about that, because I see that it is indeed true. Do not be naive to think someone is just giving freely. People are transactional in their mindset. People are Quid Pro Cuo, meaning I do for you, then you do for me. Now, with this in mind, we do not want to become cynical or untrusting of people. Do not look at everyone that does something nice for you and think "what do you really want from me?" That is a horrible way to live.

The people who love you the way you need to be loved may indeed do nice things for you, like buy you a meal or give you a gift. But, you can discern that their motive is simply to bless you and show you appreciation. How can you tell? Because they do not constantly NEED from you. They do not need your time. They do not always need your attention. A clear indicator that they do not need you is how they interact with you on Sundays at church. If they are always coming up to you to talk and to share, that shows that they need from you. Is this bad? Does this mean they are selfish and wrong? No! They probably love you and just want to be around you. That is great. But, the kind of inner circle families you need around you are people who see the burden on your shoulders to be the pastor to people on Sundays. They see that you are focused on mission, on connecting with new people. They realize that you are preparing to go up on the platform to share and that you need space to focus. The people who love you enough to give you space on Sundays and at church events are the people that you want to pursue to become inner circle families.

My inner circle families will give me a smile and a wave from a distance. When they walk by me, they will give me a fist bump or a high five, and then keep moving. They hardly ever approach me, but when I have time to go approach them, they stop and engage. These people almost always re-direct the conversation back to me and my health. They are others-focused. They love the pastor, they honor the office of pastor, and they appreciate what the pastor does for the church and the community.

I have many families that love me like this at our Christ Fellowship Stuart Campus. One family that have done this well is Steve and Sharon Addison. They started the church with me when we launched in Martin County High School with three hundred people. I was so green in leadership. I had never preached before. I was rough around the edges to say the least. Yet, Steve would find moments to let me know how much he loved me and would tell me how great I was doing. His wife, Sharon would love my wife and family with hugs and kindness.

Because we did not have many resources or facilities, the Addisons would freely open up their home for church gatherings. Sharon prepared wonderful food and Steve would make bonfires and take care of parking cars so people could join in. Steve and Sharon would always step up to lead groups, mentor people, and handle more sensitive issues with me in the church. They are well respected in the community, yet Steve and Sharon served quietly in the background. Having the Addisons stand with me as I pastor has been so vital. They lent me their credibility within the community. Before our Stuart Campus launched, our church leaders stood before the school board to get approved to rent the school. In the background, it was Steve who quietly connected with his key relationships that helped School Board Members feel more comfortable with an unknown church to come launch in their school.

To this day, I look to Steve and Sharon Addison as an inner circle family. They are not just church family. They truly have become Pilot family. They love me and all who belong to me. They are faithful, consistent, and loving. They are generous with their lives and are unassuming with their talents and success. One day years ago, I wrote down three men that I wanted to try to emulate over the next twenty years of my life. One of them was Steve Addison. I admire his faithful life. He carries tremendous influence in our church and in our community. He has great influence with me. I want to hear what Steve has to say. When we have lunch, I have to pull it out of him, because he does not like to impose his opinion on others. And he certainly does not like to talk negative.

I have seen Steve and Sharon stay planted at Christ Fellowship through transition and through change. They do not come to Christ Fellowship for what they can get out of it. They come because they are called to care for it, to ensure that it remains healthy and strong in our community. Steve and Sharon Addison are givers, not takers. They are investors, not withdrawers. When I see the Addisons at church, they smile at me and keep walking. I always want to spend more time with them, but I know on Sundays I must stay on mission. They get it. They understand.

You need people like Steve and Sharon you will love you unconditionally. You need people who get what you are doing, and why you are doing it. You need people who lift you, not people you must lift up. You need people to love your spouse, your children, and your parents. When you identify a couple like this in your church, grab them! Bring them in to your inner circle. Tell them how much you appreciate their love, their prayers, their encouragement.

Partners Who Support You

You need people who are partnering with you to shoulder the load of ministry. You need lifters. So many people in your church are needing you to lift them. But who is lifting you? Let me ask you a question, a tough question to ask: Is your staff and Elder Board lifting you up? Or do you find that you are having to lift them up? With some, you may be having to drag them along behind you. You inner circle people should be so healthy in their personal life, that they can stand with you and take the hits and lead the charge with you. You need some inner circle people who are as passionate about the church as you are.

Some people who are a part of your church may not see themselves as a partner. They see themselves as an member. People understand membership because it is evident in our society. People pay fees to credit card companies and expect to enjoy the benefits of being a member. People pay dues to country clubs and expect to be served. My wife and I pay fees to our home owners association every month. I am happy to do so, because I enjoy the amenities they provide. Every time I drive through my gated community, I pause and check to see if the flowers are blooming and the trees are trimmed. Why? Because I pay for that service, and I want to make sure it is being maintained.

I understand that when people invest their money, their time, and their gifts, they want to make sure that their church is being managed well. Understandable. So do I. But, I am drawn to people who think like a partner. A partner shoulders the burden. A partner takes personal responsibility for the health and the success of the organization. Members watch. Partners work. Members interject. Partners invest.

I have many families who embody the partner mentality at our church. One family that has been some of the greatest partners with me is Don and Sharon Jochum. They were a family that I met years ago when I was a Choir Director. They joined Christ Fellowship and joined the choir because they were great singers. They brought enthusiasm and friendship to the choir and I quickly was drawn to them. They loved singing in Choir, but when I was called to start Christ Fellowship in Martin County, they jumped on board. They would miss the Choir ministry that they loved, but they enlisted themselves on the team with me.

Don was a smart man who had started a successful business. He understood that if you want the business great, you must make it great. His wife, Sharon is right by his side and jumps in with both feet to do her part. Starting a new church means that we do not have the resources or time to do some of the fun parts of church. We had to give up the choir ministry eventually at our portable campus. To reach people in Martin County, we had to focus our attention on starting home groups. Don and Sharon embraced this like it was their own idea. They not only opened up their home, but invited people to be a part of their group. Don was always telling me how he was strategically going after people he knew he and Sharon were supposed to help connect to the church.

Don and Sharon were great partners with me. They would always attach their influence in the church to me, as their pastor. When I would go and visit their group, I saw great leadership and development of their people. They were so effective at building relationship with new people and discipling them in Jesus. Don and Sharon have become the most effective Group Leaders our Campus has! They actually have two groups that total 50 people!

Don and Sharon give more than they take. They see the church as their responsibility, their mission. They do not sit on the sidelines commenting on what they would like to see. They are too busy serving, connecting, developing. They are great partners with me, and I consider them an inner circle Family. I love them very much.

Pastors Who Extend You

Your inner circle people should echo your voice and extend your heart. These select people should reinforce your vision and be living out the church's mission. When you have people who others perceive as close to you, they can become influential to others who see the relationship you have built with them. Consequently, whoever your inner circle people connect with become vicariously connected to you, the pastor. This is why you want to make sure your inner circle are the right people, and have the right motive.

I do not categorize many who I think of as a pastor, because I realize that the mindset must be so discerning, the Biblical knowledge so vast. While some show hints of being a pastor, only a few can handle the responsibility on a high level. One man who I have been able to lean on in this way among others is Ron Brown. He and his wife, JC helped me start Stuart Campus and have been loving and supportive to me. Ron has never been a career pastor, having worked in the business world. But Ron is well-studied in God's Word, has led in church for many years, and has displayed the character and wisdom that a seasoned pastor would require.

Ron is one that can handle a tough conversation with clarity, strength, yet grace and tact. Ron can handle Bible questions and church questions, having the ability to help people understand and process to resolution. Ron also can do spiritual battle as he and his wife are prayer warriors, always prepared for whatever conflict or attack comes.

In the beginning years of our church, I recall a young man coming that I noticed was quite disturbed. We would pray for him and he showed signs of abuse and darkness. I talked with my Senior Pastor on how to handle this. We determined that there was demonic influence at work. I began to pray intensely, prepare in God's Word and thought who I could bring with me that I trusted with something of this nature. Ron Brown was who I called. Ron helped me literally cast out this demon from this young man and we witnessed this man be set free! It was a powerful experience for me.

Ron and JC have helped me navigate choppy waters with helping people through change in the church. They have helped to train up leaders in the church. They extend my leadership, because people see that we have a tight relationship. Who is your Ron Brown? Is there a retired pastor or a christian business man or woman in your midst? Maybe there is something you glean from them. They are waiting for your permission to share with you. They would love to help you, if you would just invite them in your inner circle.

How Your Inner Circle Can Work

As I said after I left the meeting with Pastor Tom, I was scratching my head thinking how this would work being more intentional to define my inner circle. With my three people, I began thinking of them differently. I saw them differently. I met with them more frequently. And, most importantly, I invited them differently.

Once you identify your inner circle, you need to prepare them for this deeper relationship you are asking of them. Obviously, before you identify your inner circle, you need to have reached a point where you feel confident that they are ready for more. You will have first needed to go through the strategy and process that I have written about thus far in this book. But now that you know who they are, you should start suggesting that you want to bring them in to your inner circle. Begin having gradual conversations with inferences where they sense that a new season and deeper relationship is on the horizon.

One thing I like to share with people who I am calling in to my inner circle is that I have been praying for key people God would give me to love me, support me and extend my ministry. I ask them to be praying for their next season and to see if they are feeling that God is calling them to more in the church.

Once you know these people are resonating with your heart, it is great to take your inner circle people out together to a special place and celebrate the great relationship you share with them. Speak in to their lives individually, and let the whole group hear the love and the value you place on each person. Then, teach how Jesus called an inner circle close to Himself. Explain to them how you need that close knit family that will stand with you and surround you. Your inner circle will rally around you like never before. It will be a sacred moment for them and for you. It will be beautiful and will be empowering!

As you begin incorporating your inner circle, you need to start engaging them in more conversation than before. One of the purposes of your inner circle is to help you carry the weight of ministry that you feel. You need to start trusting them with decisions you are facing, with tensions you are feeling. When there are people challenges in the church, you should be able to become less filtered with these people to share some of the issues you are dealing with. Ask them to pray with you and to help you solve this challenges. The whole point of trusting them is to now empower them to lead the ministry with you.

Different Circles

You may be reading through this section and are still trying to decide on who your three people are. Only three Matt?

You can actually have more than three people in your inner circle for sure. In this book, I have shared with you about many great people that I have shared ministry with. These all are part of my different inner circles. You can maybe start with three and slowly invite others to join. You can also have a few inner circles. Yes – you can form a few circles of friends or leaders or mentors together separate from other circles. These inner circles will be formed on common interests, common age group, common position in ministry.

I had my Adam, Travis and Talena as an inner circle who were on staff with me for years at the Stuart Campus. They became the team that helped me think through strategy, creativity, and people at the church. As a result of working closely together, we created a strong bond of community. We shared jokes and fun. We would celebrate each other with wins at work and joys in our personal lives. We became a support group for each other, cheering each other on. We also had enough trust that we could argue and debate while maintaining relationship.

This inner circle worked so well for me, that I eventually created a second inner circle with some key families in our church. If I could have three like Jesus, I could also have twelve like Jesus. Different layers of different circles.

Two families that I invited in to this relationship were the Chittys and the Agulias, whom I mentioned earlier. Creating this deeper circle with them and others pulled them in to building the culture and the health of our Campus. There are key families in my church who have a true ministry call on their lives, but they are not able to fully commit to working at the church. Bringing them in to your inner circle gives them permission to live out their calling to build the church.

These couples were the twelve people that were in the front row every service. They led projects and outreaches. They were the best connectors of people and helped me know who I should be connecting with as the pastor. These people were lifters to me and my wife, and they loved us well. I never felt like I was alone as the pastor because these families stood with me and full support.

Different Circles for Different Seasons

As years move on, people will likely transition from the church. My inner circle of Adam, Travis and Talena changed because each of them moved to a new place of leadership. I hated to see them leave my team, but I was so proud of each of them. We would remain close friends, but my inner circle was no longer. I needed to start again. I needed to re-assess what I needed, and who I needed.

The same goes for some of the inner circles I have created with families in my church. Some of them are leading other business ventures and have other priorities in their life. We remain close and they still serve in the church and love me. But I knew that I needed to form other inner circles for this season of my life.

Conclusion

Just as I am taking the time even now to pray and to seek out inner circle people, you need to do the same. You will need to re-assess who you need close around you. Learn to see people as different layers around you. Different circles. You can have many inner circles, and that is a great sign that you are attractional and you are relational. But you need to define who are your three? Who are your twelve?

Thus far, I have focused on how a pastor cares for, builds up and develops people. As a Strategic Pastor, you should give most of your focus to people. You are in the people business, and you need to remember that you are not building a church, you are building people. People are the church. As we move on in our study of a Strategic Pastor, we will begin to see how we can build the church. Church growth and expansion of ministry reach is always at the forefront of every passionate pastor. Healthy things grow. God wants your church to grow and to flourish. Let's look at the ways we you accomplish that.

Chapter 6   Inner Circle

Study Questions

Who are people who could become your inner circle? Take a
moment and list out at least two people that fit each category:

People who love you

_____

_____

Partners who support you

_____

_____

Pastors who extend you

_____

_____

What spaces of time could work in the next few weeks to get with
your inner circle for a retreat or a dinner? List them now. If you
buy in to the importance of having an inner circle, you will prioritize this planning above other work in your church and ministry.

What season are you in as a pastor? Describe it. Next, define
what kind of inner circle you need for this season.

Chapter 7

How to Build a Church

Do you have to have a big church to be effective? Do you have to be bigger than the church down the road? Is it possible to be too big as a church?

The measurement we should look at is not how big our church is, but how much our church is growing. This metric will be an outcome of another, which is how healthy your church is. You see, the Church is more than just an organization. It is a living, breathing organism. When you think of a plant, you begin to see the delicate, living creation that will thrive, but only under the right conditions. A plant would not just stay the same size. It would not continue looking the same. It is always changing, always becoming something greater. Most plants produce seeds that have the potential to become other plants.

> The measurement we should look at is not how big our church is, but how much our church is growing.

My conviction is that a healthy church should be growing. It should be growing numerically, financially, and spiritually. More growth translates in to greater reach and impact. A healthy church should have an outflow of leaders, pastors, missionaries, singers, business owners, and teachers who are living out their calling. I believe the pastor's charge is not to just care for the church; he should intentionally work to **BUILD** the church. Jesus did not start the church to just manage it; He came to **BUILD** it:

Matthew 16:18
... upon this rock I will **BUILD** my church, and all the powers of hell will not prevail against it.

Jesus did not focus on caring for the church. He did not focus on teaching the church. He did not focus on saving the church. All of those things, He did. However, He emphasized **building** the church. God is a Master Builder. He has a design that is intentional. His purpose is to take us somewhere. Could you imagine if God's plan stopped with just saving the people of Israel? All of the nations of the world would be lost. We would never be included in God's divine plan as the Church. God had a bigger plan in store to save all nations and creeds through the nation of Israel. His plan was Jesus. And Jesus' strategy was through the Church! As Strategic Pastors, we need to follow God's design and become master builders, building His Church and expanding His reach. We need to embrace that mindset. Move away from doing the work of a manager and curator. Begin to shift to the greater work of designer and builder.

What is the Church?

What is the Church to you? How do you describe the Church? If you are part of a church, you may think you understand what it is. But how do people who aren't associated with a church view it? To understand what the Church is, or should be, it is worth looking at it through the lense of how others see. What word would they use to describe "Church?"

In one of my team meetings, I had a guest speaker come do a leadership lesson. She made us think about this question when did a word association exercise. She told us that she would present a word, and then invited us to respond with the first word that came to mind. She shared the following words and we responded:

Starbucks...everyone said "coffee"
Toyota...everyone shouted "car"
Legos....everyone answered "toy"
Church....some said, "Jesus", "building", "people", "Christians", "God", "cross", "family", "Sunday service"

Wow! We all looked at each other as we realized that we all have different ideas and images of what the Church is. The lady made the point of the lesson: if we as the Church Leaders were unclear of what the Church is, then people outside the church MUST be unclear!

The word, Church comes from the Greek word, Ekklesia, which describes a group of faithful people who follow Jesus Christ and represent Him on the Earth. The Bible teaches that this group of believers is literally the body of Christ on Earth, whose mission is to fulfill God's purpose of sharing about Jesus to all people, with the hope that they will follow Him.

As I thought about the Church, as I would define it in **one word**, I decided I would land on:

Family

I know using just one word to describe the Church can be dangerous theologically. I mean the Church is the Bride of Christ. The Church is not JUST a family of ANYONE. One must be a blood-bought follower of Jesus Christ who has their name written in the Lamb's book of Life in Heaven. I know there is so much that needs to be clarified to stay true to God's purpose for His Church. But, for the purpose of trying to encapsulate all that the Church is for someone who does not understand the Theology of the Church, I want to create a clear image for people grasp. The word **"family"** I believe is a beautiful picture that portrays the heart of Jesus for His Church.

Building People

Family is all about people. The reason why I pick the word "family" is that it draws our attention away from the building, or the church service. Family does not take your mind to theology or ministries. Family focuses on people. Family paints a beautiful picture. If someone would ask "what is a church", and you respond "it is a family you can belong to", that communicates something that people can see, and that everyone longs for.

> The church is people. If we focus on building people's lives, then the church will naturally grow as a result.

I tell myself often that I am not building a church, I am building people. Why do I say this? Because I have already mentioned that I am a success-driven, goal-oriented person and I like to win. I like to build. And yet, I have to remind myself that the church is not a competition. It is not a goal to grow. It is not a project to accomplish. It is people. The church is people. If I focus on building people's lives, then the church will naturally grow as a result.

People do not all fit neatly in my paradigm of what I think church should look like in a perfect scenario. My job is to make a place for all kinds of people, wherever they are in their journey to know God. I want to help them fit in and belong in God's family. When I learn to love people and help them grow in Christ, I get to partner with the Holy Spirit as He heals their wounds, teaches them, and grows them up to become more like Jesus. Seeing people belong, heal, and grow is the most beautiful thing I get to be a part of as a pastor in our church. Seeing people become what God intends for them is what "Church" should be all about.

If you are willing to change your paradigm of how you build the church, from building organization to building people, you will need to grow in the following attributes:

Patience
Growing people takes patience. I like to call this painful patience. Driven leaders want results fast. Systematic leaders want processes to flow exactly as their master plan dictates. People, however, take time to grow, time to become. With people, it takes you helping them forward with one step, only to see them take two steps backwards. You help an alcoholic learn steps to stay sober for three months, only for them to relapse. You help a man learn to be loving and kind to his wife, only to hear that he blew up at her again. You have to ask God to grow your patience, so you can give a lot of grace to people. Give people the gift of time and you will watch them grow healthier.

Perspective
Some people manifest bad behavior or a bad attitude. Negativity, arguing, gossiping are common with people. But before you begin quoting every scripture to them about not gossiping or not attacking, learn to gain some perspective with people. Where is this bad behavior stemming from? What is the root cause of it? What have they been through that causes them to react this way? What was their upbringing? Because we are building people, we want to think like a doctor who studies the patient and identifies the cause of the symptom.

I am not saying we excuse bad behavior. But I am saying you need to ask the Holy Spirit to give you discernment on what is really going on the inside of people. Author and Pastor, Lance Witt says "listen for the ten percent that people are not telling you." When you address what the root cause is, the bad behavior will fall away.

Progress
One attribute I have always had is that I tend to see the positive. I see the best in people. There is a famous truth that says we judge others by their actions while we want to be judged by our intentions. I truly believe that people want to do good. They want to be their best. But because they are growing and becoming, they will struggle with old habits and fail.

Learn to focus on people's progress. Point to where they are winning, even if it is hard to see. Pastor Julie Mullins teaches our leaders at Christ Fellowship to walk around and catch people doing good. And then, celebrate them. I love that. Why? Because when you focus on their progress, they will repeat what you celebrate, and intuitively drop what is not celebrated.

Building the Church

How do you build your church? How do you grow it?

If you are currently a pastor of a church, you likely have hit a lid of growth at some point. Maybe you are hitting that lid right now. I talk with so many great pastors who are gifted, who are passionate, and committed. They are doing such great work and are doing many things well. But they feel defeated when they can't move the needle to get their church pressing forward. The tendency is to just work harder, just do more. But if you are a pastor, I would bet that you are already running at full capacity. You really do not have any more to give. Pastors are the hardest workers out there. What else could you possibly do?

The first thing I want to do in addressing church growth is to point back to all of the previous chapters I have been talking about. If you focus on people, and you are strategic about loving people, building teams and developing leaders, your church will grow. This principal alone will allow the church to grow naturally.

Allow it to Grow

What has helped me grow my church time and time again is not "building" the church, per se. The secret I will share with you is: we do not have the ability to grow the church. Rather, what I CAN DO is to make sure the church is healthy and strong so that it will be **allowed to grow**.

> # Make sure the church is healthy and strong so that it will be allowed to grow.

I remember learning this principle when every year I would have to set growth goals for our Stuart Campus. I would have to stand in front our Leadership Team and present an audacious, bold plan to grow the attendance, grow the volunteer teams, and grow the amount of giving that would fund our Campus. In preparing the plan, I would sit in my office staring at my whiteboard thinking "what can I possibly do to make more people attend? How am I going to push people to serve more? How do I find more people who will tithe at my Campus?" Talk about overwhelming.

When we feel the pressure to grow the church, we immediately think of solutions like bringing in special guests, providing better weekend experience, making investments in facilities and staff. While I believe there is a time and place to plan for those pieces, I would urge you to go back to the fundamentals of my Triple Threat Process I have been describing. I know they are not exciting or sparkly. And they will NOT bring immediate results. That is important to be reminded of, and essential to communicate to your Elder Board and Leader teams. Hey, nothing that you accomplish in life happens suddenly. Success is not a one-time event. Pat Riley, Coach of the Los Angeles Lakers teaches "Success is the daily pursuit of excellence." You don't lose thirty pounds with one day of fasting and working out in the gym. You lose thirty pounds by practicing attainable objectives consistently over time.

As I have led my Campus at Christ Fellowship, I have been so blessed by God that every year, we have seen growth. Growth numerically, growth financially, growth in salvations, in volunteers, in partnerships. God has made our Campus grow. Even when other Campuses have been birthed near us and people left us to go launch, we grew back again. It has amazed me! We have reached our goals every year, and even beyond! It has not been because I worked harder or had some creative idea. It has been my faithfulness to God and my practicing the Triple Threat Process of loving people, building teams and developing leaders.

Change your mindset from having big vision weekends or bringing in expensive speakers or music artists. **Stop trying to draw a crowd and start working to create a church family.**

> Stop trying to draw a crowd and start working to create a church family.

Healthy people translate to a healthy church. A healthy church translates in to a growing church. Growth happens naturally. We do not have to push something to grow. Rather, our focus should be like that of a gardener. We tend the soil, we fertilize the plant. We make sure the plants get enough water and sun. We protect the plants against disease. Healthy things grow.

I began applying this kind of thinking with our Stuart Campus. Rather than trying to grow things, I tried to make things healthy. As a result, we hit our goals EVERY YEAR. We usually moved BEYOND our stated goals. If you grow your people, they will become your greatest billboards through the community. They will happily invite their friends to their church because they love to share how they are growing. When your people are happy, their natural action will be to invest themselves in THEIR church (not THE church.) They will jump in with great enthusiasm. Healthy people want to work, they want to build, they want to dream and achieve. People who are bought in want other people to buy in. Your greatest resource in ministry is your people. Harness their passion and their ingenuity.

Listen to me: I am not saying to just sit back and let it happen. Remember that you are to become more strategic, more intentional with your focus, your words and your time. I want to teach you to become *outward-focused* to propel your church to greater impact.

Magnetic Pull

There is a magnetic pull on you, pastor. Do you feel it?
Every pastor has a magnetic pull inward to the church. The people, the needs, and the ministries are always pulling you in for your attention. People want more of your time and attention.

This keeps your focus inward, not allowing you to see beyond the church. To help your church reach greater impact, you must RESIST this pull. Stretch outward. Reach outside the church. Let me balance this with all that I have taught previously. I have thus far talked about loving and shepherding people. I have taught on building teams and developing leaders. I have emphasized the need to work to build a healthy culture within your church. This all takes focusing inward.

This will be a tension that you will have to manage. However, in order for your church be what Jesus intends for it to be, there needs to be some energy and time reserved and carved out for you as the pastor to look outward in your community. The great news is, however, that the more you create a strong and healthy culture within the church, the more margin you will create for yourself to invest outward. When your church is healthy and growing, there are far less problems you have to solve. You find that you do not have to re-communicate vision or directives over and over again. You have leaders who are reinforcing your voice to the people.

Pastor, you need to resist the magnetic pull inward to the church so you can lead the church outward in your community. As you begin focusing some time outside the church, you will catapult your church forward in growth and impact. Here is how:

Partnerships

One of the best things you can give your time to is to look for great leaders and organizations within your community that you can build relationship with. Look for partnerships with people that have proven success and who share common vision and culture that you have in your church. Partnerships are powerful. They are explosive. When your church joins with a great organization that is doing something great in the community, it becomes a symbiotic relationship. Your church can offer something they do not have which is volunteers and finances. And they have something you may not have, which is community presence and networking outside your church.

When your church people are growing healthy, you will find that they are looking for even greater ways to serve and have impact. That is a great "problem" for a pastor to have! But it does become a challenge when you need to create opportunities for greater impact. Looking outside the church will help you find opportunities for your people to be the church outside of the church. This will make your church culture even more healthy than it already is. It gives your people a sense of impact and purpose. High capacity people are drawn to solving challenges in their community. I have people who are attracted to our church, Christ Fellowship mainly because they love that we serve locally!

Conclusion

There is so much more I could show you in how partnerships will catapult you and your church to higher impact. When you are seen in the community as serving, it communicates to people outside your church that you exist and that you are on mission. People love this. You get to serve in communities where unchurched people live. Your church family will actually be interacting with the very people who need Jesus in their life. This becomes a missions field!

In the next chapter, I expand on focusing your attention outward to people outside your church family. This concept was so foreign to me, and I think it seems illogical to most pastors. Because pastors think of themselves as the Shepherd over their flock, thinking outward seems like an after-thought. But You will see how focusing outward will put you on a platform that you never thought possible. God wants to use you in such a bigger way.

Chapter 7   How to Build Your Church

Study Questions

What would you say are the growing indicators of your church? In which areas does your church need to grow in? In which areas are you seeing healthy growth?

When you think of the definition of church, what one word comes to mind? Do the exercise described in this chapter with you staff. Do it also with a group of people within your church. Do word associations, and then, present the word "church", and listen to their responses and observe their reactions. You will learn a lot about what everyone perceives is the church, and what her purpose is.

Describe the magnetic pull you feel as a pastor, that is of your church people and of the needs and responsibility of leading the church. What pulls at you? What do you know you need to do more of outside the church, in order for the church to be what God intends for her to be?

Chapter 8

Pastor your Community

As we begin to see our church grow strong and healthy, we create margin to focus outward in the community. As we are begin serving people in the community and build partnerships with leaders and organizations, we begin to earn influence with them. Serving people is the quickest way to earn trust. Loving people is the quickest way to build relationship.

I learned to become more community-minded from my pastor at Christ Fellowship, Todd Mullins. Pastor Todd is a tremendous Pastor and Leader – the best. He has a passion for God and carries a burden for his calling to serve our church. I heard him share his burden one day and it gripped my heart. He said "I realize that I am not just called to pastor Christ Fellowship, I am called to pastor this region." Wow – what a responsibility. And knowing the humility of Todd, I know he was not seeking out that huge assignment. He has shared a Bible verse with his staff, one that Todd said he grew up learning in his home. It is found in in Luke 12:48:

...to whom much is given, much is required.

The Mullins family understand that God has blessed Christ Fellowship with growth and impact. With that blessing, however comes a responsibility. They feel a responsibility to bring leadership to this region, and to create partnership and unity with churches and organizations.   God's favor is on us, but it's not just *for* us.

I took this statement that Pastor Todd shared and personalized it for me. I was entrusted to look after the Stuart Campus in Martin County. But, there was more. I was now going to start enlarging my sphere of reach to Martin County. This changed how I

> God's favor is on us, but it's not just *for* us.

viewed our Martin County region. I began getting a burden for the pastors of nearby churches. I began thinking how I could support the School District, where we had rented High Schools for seven years. I began thinking about the Sheriff's office. I started saying yes to requests from Non-profit ministry organizations.

While I began taking on this role of pastoring our Martin County region, I did not tell everyone this. The last thing I want to do is to declare myself the high position of "Regional Pastor." I hate leading from position. I much prefer to lead through serving and partnering. To clarify, God did not give me this burden early on as a pastor starting out. I was not ready for it. Taking on more pastoral responsibility means that you have been leading successfully in your church for a number of years. It means that all systems are running and that your church is serving in the community. This was a next step in my leadership and in my calling by God for our region.

If you feel you may be in a season where you are on cruise control, where you feel a bit under-challenged, step out in to this expanded role. It will be a next level of leadership and impact. If done well, it will actually come back to help your church grow. How? I cannot quite explain how that works, actually. I have given some of our best talent and resources to other churches with nothing given in return. I guess it goes back to the Biblical principle:

Luke 6:38
Give, and it will be given to you. A good measure, pressed down, shaken together and running over, will be poured into your lap. For with the measure you use, it will be measured to you.

God's math on your return on investment is unfair. It is unbalanced. And it's in YOUR favor. This statement in Luke Chapter 6 does not just promise to make good on returning back to you what you have given. That would be transactional. For instance, if I give $100, I will receive $100. If I serve someone in the community, I will then receive a like gift from someone. No, God's way of returning the blessing is with "good measure, pressed down, shaken together and running over." That is a very detailed explanation of how God prepares His blessing for those who give on behalf of Him.

> God's math on your return on investment is unfair. And it's in YOUR favor.

Why does God give such a vivid, detailed picture for us on how God will return what we give? Because God knows that we are concerned about our wellbeing. We are interested in what we can accomplish and what we can gain. God wants to assure you and I that when we give to God, and on behalf of God, He will greatly reward us. A great act of faith will result in a great reward!

So, if this Biblical principle is true, why do we then as pastors become territorial with our churches? Why do we withhold resources? Why are we slow to help and serve other churches? Do we just believe in this giving principle with our personal tithe, our personal serving with friends and family, but then see our leadership within our church and ministry as something different?

Territorial

I have heard of too many pastors who were upset with other pastors because their church was stealing "their people." I have never really bought in to that concept of "their people." Most pastors do not set out to steal people from other churches. Most pastors are not secretly bent on trying to destroy other churches in order to build their own. pastors I know are so full of compassion for the lost, for the hurting and the broken, that they are working hard to reaching these people.   Pastors I know are sacrificing in every area of their life, putting people's needs before their own so that they can be fully available to how God wants to use them.

When I hear rumblings within the community that one church is "stealing people", I don't believe it. First, we as pastors do not "own" people. We have no right to claim people. While we have a responsibility to care for them and develop them in their walk to follow Jesus, we must be careful not have a possessive mentality. Jesus did not have a possessive, owner mindset with His disciples. We see in Scripture how Jesus prayed for His disciples whom He cared for. But He always remembered that they did not belong to Him, but to God:

John 17:6-8 NIV
I have revealed you to those whom you gave me out of the world. They were yours; you gave them to me and they have obeyed your word. Now they know that everything you have given me comes from you. For I gave them the words you gave me and they accepted them. They knew with certainty that I came from you, and they believed that you sent me.

Always remember who your people belong to. It is God who gave them to your care.   You do not own them. You do not control them. If they choose to move away, let them go. If they are drawn to another church, let them go. Do not make them feel pressure or guilt for leaving. In fact, if you want to win them over, use these times as opportunities to prove your genuine care for them. It is how you respond that will reveal your true heart. Your leadership will be tested in these moments with people, with the community, and with other churches. Don't hold them down – lift them up. Release them with your blessing. Thank them for their investment in the church, however big it was or little it was. Tell them they will always have a church home with you. Tell them that you love them and that you appreciate them. You will leave a lasting impression of love and care on their life. Whether they leave or stay is not your responsibility. Your responsibility is to pastor them. Leave them in God's hands. They belong to God.

Pastor to Pastor

As we discuss how it looks to pastor your community, I want to first address how you ought to interact with other pastors and Churches. While we will get to being a pastor to people outside church, we need to start with other pastors. Why? Because how we relate with our counterpart pastors in our community directly affects how the community perceives our church. Jesus was all about unity within the church. And He was not just referring to a single church body. He was referring to the big "C" church, meaning all people who profess their faith in Jesus Christ on the Earth today.

John 13:35
They will know you are my disciples by this: if you love one another.

Pastoring the community starts with being a pastor to other pastors and church leaders. You must remember that being a pastor is a scary, daunting task. Pastors are living on faith every day. They are in a spiritual war zone and feel they do not have enough money, wisdom or resources. As a pastor, you should know this above all. If you think you have stress and challenges at your church, think of the pastor who has even less resources and people than you do.

Local pastors need to bond together, not compete with one another. Pastors are to be cheerleading one another, encouraging one another. When a pastor is experiencing victory and seeing fruit in their church, you ought to be the first to celebrate and brag on them. When a pastor is struggling or has a had a failure, you should be the first to come alongside to protect, defend and support.

> Local Pastors need to bond together, not compete with one another.

Even Pastors Need a Pastor

No one can encourage a pastor like another pastor. Think about that statement. No one has the ability to affirm and encourage a pastor more than someone who understands, who has been there before. While people in their congregation can certainly encourage and affirm, it means more coming from a local pastor. If you have had any success in being a pastor, you likely have great people skills. You must have become effective in giving inspiration and timely encouragement. You can express love with words and with care like few people have the ability to do. Use it freely with other pastors and Church Leaders!

There have been seasons I went through where I needed a Pastor in my life. Certainly, I have had many great Pastors at Christ Fellowship who have loved and supported me, above all the Mullins family who I have mentioned throughout this book. But there was a Pastor who moved to Martin County to retire. His family was a part of Christ Fellowship Stuart Campus, and he and his wife made our church their church home. I had visited Max Yeary's church playing the piano for a musical gathering. It was a great church that had great impact in South Florida. I was so thankful now to actually have this Pastor a part of our congregation in Stuart!

There was a time when I was wrestling with my dreams and my gifts to be a Pastor. Yes, I have doubted my calling and questioned my future, just like you have. I remember running in to Max after church one day. I was trying to "Pastor" him, by greeting him and checking in with him. He could tell something was wrong in me. Because we had built a relationship, he began to ask some questions, and then, he just listened. We ended up having lunch that week. Max began sharing with me his journey as a Pastor. He could describe exactly what I was feeling and could explain why I was feeling it. I was able to express myself to him in a protected way that was so relieving. He understood. And he knew how to handle what I was sharing with him.

Pastor Max Pastored me. Max tells me not to call him Pastor at church, because he likes the thought of being retired. It's a fun joke we share between us. He always calls me Pastor, I think to remind me that now I have the responsibility of Pastor. Max and his wife, Ophelia go out of their way to love me and my entire family. They text, they love, they care, the brag on, and they pray. Anything I ask them to do in the church, they do with joy and dedication. I am so glad God sent a Pastor and his precious family to Pastor me and my family.

As a pastor in your community, you have the unique gift of speaking right to the heart and to the need of another pastor. You can say what others cannot express. You can point out what others do not see. You can speak from hands-on experience. You need to ask God who are a few pastors in your community that you should invest your life in to. This is truly the heart of God.

Getting practical with Pastors

So how on earth do you get connected with pastors within your community? And how do you care for them in a way that they will receive it, and not resist it?

The most direct way I do this is simply to pick up the phone and call their church. I ask to meet them for lunch or coffee. I tell them up front that I have no agenda except to build a relationship with them. I will make statements like "I am so glad you are pastoring here in Martin County." "Martin County needs you." "I hope you pastor here for many years, and I want to see your church grow and reach many people." If I do get time with them face to face, that is best. I ask about their family. I ask about their church. I ask about their background and their life journey. I make it all about them. If they ask about me, I share about our church and my life. However, I refrain from sharing how big the church is, or how many paid staff I have working with me. Only if they ask, will I share those specifics.

One thing I do in the conversation is regulate how much I am talking to how much they are talking. I try to keep an 80%/20%

ratio, with them at 80% and me at 20%. This interaction needs to be about giving to them, not taking from them. Don't try to teach or coach. Don't try to warn them of the dangers of the community. Don't monopolize with stories and statistics. Listen. With your eyes. With your body language. Put your smart phone down. Sit comfortably, like you are not in a hurry to leave. Give them your attention.

Another way I show care and encouragement to community pastors is through Social Media. I will find their Social Media accounts online and begin to celebrate their posts. I will make quick comments like "I love this pastor." "This is such a great church in our community." "Christ Fellowship loves this church – we are with you!" I have seen pastors who I previous had little connection with warm up to me after seeing some of these posts. Some pastors now have reciprocated on Social Media and like my posts! How awesome. This is seen not only by the pastor, but by everyone who follows our posts. This makes a huge statement about your church, their church, and THE CHURCH to the community.

Yet another way I build relationship and show care to pastors is around Christmas and Easter. With all of the pastors I have built any relationship with, I will send them a quick text the week of Easter or Christmas. I send the text usually to the pastors individually, rather than send a group text. The reason I do this is that I do not want to give off the perception that I am the "Area leader of pastors." This can seem arrogant and unwanted. Rather, I send a note of encouragement individually, as a friend would send to a friend. I find when I do this, even the most busy pastors respond back with thanks. And, because I sent the text messages individually, sometimes I get a prayer request back. When the pastor feels safe and guarded with his relationship with you, he will open up to you.

Yes, pastors are people just like you. They have stress, anxiety, sin issues. They have huge responsibilities and pressures put on them. With their big Easter weekend or Christmas services looming, a quick text of encouragement can go a long way. There is a pastor that needs a timely word from you today. Get his cell number. Or, get his e-mail. If you can't get that, send a note to the church receptionist. Send an e-mail to the generic e-mail on the website – info@............ .org. I have done that myself. And I eventually heard from the pastor. Find ways you can communicate care and love to local pastors.

Local Leaders and Officials

In the same way that you may not naturally think to reach out to local pastors, you may forget to reach out to your Local Leaders. Sheriffs are people who need relationship. Politicians need encouragement. School Board Members, County Commissioners, School Principals would appreciate some support from you. Trying to build a relationship with these people will feel intimidating for sure. I know when I started our church in Martin County, I felt so inferior, so un-important that I would never think to approach the local Sheriff or a County Commissioner. But as I became more familiar with the "who's who" of our community, I felt more comfortable with approaching them and introducing myself. I was surprised to find that when I started talking with them, they were actually very kind, very real and very humble. I found that people in these key leadership positions had a servant-mindset themselves. They were not bothered to meet me. Rather, they saw it as their job to serve me. Wow! I was amazed. Once I had interacted with them, I now had built a bridge to them. I had broken past the church "bubble" that I lived in to expand my circle within the community. I was in!

Slow and Strategic

Now listen up. I want to teach you something here. This will help you, if you are willing to listen and learn. If you are a driven leader who wants to see things happen fast, you need to particularly pay attention.

When you meet a community leader like a Sheriff, a Politician, don't go in for a kill. What do I mean by that? When you finally get to meet them, your driven tendency will be to seize the opportunity to tell them your vision and to try to get them to work together with you. Or, maybe you are needing an in-road within the political system and need some help in getting past red tape. Don't do it. Resist this temptation. Don't let your first impression be that of aggressive vision, personal agenda, and requests.

Think about how you view people in your church who make a bee line for you. They see you that are the pastor, the person in charge. They walk so fast towards you, you think they are going to run you over. They talk big and they talk loud. They begin vision-casting and name-dropping. They give you suggestions on what you should do in the church. After they are done pouring out all of their ideas and successes, they ask you "hey, can we get together soon for lunch to talk more about this?" If you are like me, you walk the other way when you see people like I just described. Tell me, is this the kind of person you welcome in to your inner circle? Maybe you do, but not me. No sir. Run, Forest, Run!

I am drawn to people who are quietly great. I like people who hide their success. I am attracted to people who are lifters of others. They are busy making an impact. They are faithful where they are. I love people who simply want to add value to me, to encourage me. When I am around people who show an interest in my wellbeing, I want to grow closer to them. We return to the people who love us best.

So, be this kind of a leader to the Community Leaders you meet. The first interaction is probably the most important to set the tone. Back off. Back away. Use the same 80%/20% with them that I mentioned earlier. Be about them, not about you. Sure, you have that huge barrier with a permit for your church building you need approved. Of course, you already have an agenda to ask the school to let you have an event on their campus. But this is not the time, not the place. Slow down. Be strategic.

The next step is to follow up with a note sent to their office. As a pastor, you can take the conversation spiritual. They expect it from a pastor, so use that. You can offer your pastoral support to them. This is where pastoring your community really works well. Whether they go to another church or no church is inconsequential. This is your opportunity to show genuine care and attention to them. Remember that likely no other pastor or leader is caring for them well. I told you the story of my dad in his church for a reason. Only YOU have that God-given ability to encourage, to care and to affirm their leadership. You are not trying to get them to follow your leadership. People follow those who invest in them the most. But you will be able to get them to catch your heart for the community.

> **People follow those who invest in them the most.**

When you do in fact need to get something done within the community, and it involves a Leader that you have built relationship with, let me give you another piece of advice: WORK WITHIN THE SYSTEM. DO NOT pick up the phone and call them directly. Do not text them. Believe me when I tell you that you are likely burning a bridge of relationship that is so delicate. Do not put pressure on them to do you favors. I don't care how close you are to them. You may have just had lunch with a leader recently. Or, they may have served with you on a community project. Don't mistake that familiarity with a favor.

When you seek to get needed approvals, or need to get business done, go through the proper channels. When you do, you make a big statement to them. That is, you play fair. You are making it easy on them. You are saying to them that you do not expect any special favors. It may take longer than you would want. It may get stuck with one of their middle managers. You may have a tough customer you are dealing with, and they are not even aware of it. But it would be much better for them to learn of this from their end, than from your end. Don't complain. Don't cause them undo stress. Rather – SERVE them. Wait patiently. Let process play out.

When you go through the proper channels, and the channels get stuck, you will find that they will cut red tape, if you have added value to the leader first. They will help you in bigger ways than you could ever have hoped for. Great things happen when you honor the relationship of regulation. Slow down. Be strategic.

Remember that the goal is not to get the permit approved. It is not to get the access granted for your event. The greater goal is building relationship. The bigger win is that community leaders perceive you as helpful, caring, and as serving them. Go slow in the beginning, serve along the way, and you will see greater success for years to come.

Serve in the Community

The most impactul way you can be a pastor to the community is to serve in the community. Whether you create your own opportunity, or an opportunity presents itself, you need to apportion some of your time to serve at community events. There is no greater way to share the heart of your church in the community than to serve people. Serving people is a common theme in this book, because it was a common theme in the leadership of Jesus. People take notice of those who show up to serve.

I have already touched on ideas like creating Saturday serve projects for your church family to be a part of. Sometimes, it is powerful to have you and your staff show up to someone else's community project and just serve. Don't lead it, just serve at it. This makes a huge statement that you are willing to partner with what their organization is already doing.

When you have intentionally built relationship with the Sherriff's Department, they will call you in a crisis. You will have a front seat to caring for a family and supporting the Sheriff's department. When you have built rapport with the School Board and a local school, they will call you when there is a crisis at the school. You will be invited in to a community situation where you can pray, lead and care for many families and teachers. Be quick to respond to these opportunities. Create margin at the church so that you can be available immediately when you get the call. This is why I have spent so much time in this book on strategically building teams and developing leaders within your church. You need plenty of margin to be available to the community

Conclusion

As a pastor, think bigger. Think beyond. While you are to shepherd your church, God has also placed you in the community. What good is your church being in the community if she is not impacting the community? The best marketing for your church is not the use of billboards and mail outs. Don't waste the limited budget of your church. Your best marketing is how well you pastor your community.

As a Strategic Pastor, there is much that you will learn to delegate. Pastoring your community is not something you ought to delegate. You are the pastor. You are the face of the church. When you show up in the community, you make a statement - not just for you, but for your church. Actually, you make a statement about the heart of God. When you serve in the community, you prove that the church is alive and relevant. The church is the answer to solving the problems in our culture. We can't do everything, but we can do something. And that something has great impact when you respond quickly and respond well.

In this next chapter, we will deal with the problems we face with people. You only have to be a pastor for twenty-four hours to realize that when you deal with people, you will deal with problems. Let's learn strategically how we can navigate well through these problems.

Chapter 8   Pastor Your Community

Study Questions

On a scale of 1 – 10, how do you rate yourself as being church-mind-ed versus community – minded? Name a couple of ways recently that you have been a pastor to your community.

What pastors in your community are already doing this well, that is, being a pastor in your community? How are you going to start working together with them to be a part of serving in the community? If there is nobody really doing this well, you may need to initiate some ways to serve!

Do you know any local officials? List the names of the following in your community. Next to their name, mark either a check mark saying that you have a relationship with them, or an x mark saying that you do not know them. Make a plan this year to build a relationship with each person with an x.

Sheriff   _____

Police Chief   _____

School Board Member   _____

County Commissioner   _____

Mayor   _____

School Principal   _____

Congressman   _____

Ministry Organization   _____

Another Pastor   _____

Chapter 9

People Problems

A tired pastor met with his Elder board after church one Sunday and complained "you know, pastoring would be so much easier if it weren't for all of the people."

I hope in this book you can pick up that being a pastor is ALL ABOUT people. And it's not always the great people, or the easy people. You won't get to spend time just with the healthy, positive, supportive people. I grew up in my father's church as a young boy learning the illustration using my hands "here's the church, here's the steeple. Open up the doors and...there's all the people." That's right. ALL of them. The broken ones. The negative ones. You'll find runaway Rhonda and saintly Sam. You'll find hooked-on-heroin Hank, and holier-than-thou Harriett. God will send you all kinds of people with all types of hurts, hang ups, and habits. You will be dealing with people who are at different stages of their growth and their relationship with God.

As a Strategic Pastor, I have coached you to limit your time with the broken, and focus on the high capacity people and the people that show potential. The reason is that you are to care for every person that God sends to your church. The best way to do this is by building a team and raising up leaders who can help you care for everyone. But even your best people are still people. Do not be surprised that people will stumble and fall. Do not be discouraged that people quit or question. They are people, plain and simple. When you remember that a pastor is a Shepherd, then what does that make your people?

Sheep.

Bah ah ah

As a Shepherd, you must have compassion for people. You must be quick to extend grace. You must take time to understand people's tendencies and weaknesses. Jesus modeled this for us:

Matthew 9:36 ESV
Seeing the people, He felt compassion for them, because they were distressed and dispirited like sheep without a shepherd.

See people the way Jesus sees them. See them as sheep who need a shepherd. See their need for love, for direction, for support. That is your job as the pastor, the Shepherd. There will be days that you will lose patience with people. Moses did. He lost patience with the children of Israel. But keep the perspective of God always in your heart. God has compassion and understanding that we are weak and broken. We are in need of a Shepherd who will lead them to the one who can meet every need they have, Jesus Christ.

Psalm 23
The Lord is my Shepherd. I shall not be in want.

In this chapter, I want touch on some of the common problems we will deal with when interacting with people. If we can better understand why people do what they do, why people think how they think, then we will handle decisions better.

Dealing With Change

The first, and most common challenge you will have in dealing with people is when change is happening. Change is difficult to go through. Most people do not like change. Nobody likes change when it feels forced on them. And yet, in order for the church to accomplish her mission, she must change, continually.

People are dealing with change in their personal lives. They are getting older, not younger. Culture is changing at a rapid pace. People around them are changing. Change creates stress. Change implies that they do not have full control of their surroundings, or their circumstances. So, when you as the pastor introduce change in the church, do not be surprised when people react negatively. Understand the pain they feel when something that they thought would stay the same is moved in their life.

In 1998, Author Dr. Spencer Johnson wrote a little story book titled "Who Moved My Cheese?" This book has become a classic in business management, as it deals with the concept of understanding the impact of change for people. It tells the story of how a couple of mice find that the cheese they eat has been moved from its usual position. This creates anxiety for both of them. It shows how one mouse handles the change poorly, while the other one finds a way to locate some other cheese.

While this book is a cute caper of finding the cheese, it hits the nerve for identifying the cause of pain when people deal with change. I noticed that this book was written in 1998, not far from a big change coming at the turn of the century to 2000. I remember the scare in the world was Y2K. At the time, people thought the world was going to end, because all computer system clocks were going to flip on January 1, 2000 causing a worldwide crash. No wonder Dr. Johnson was thinking about how to deal with change!

Help People Process

As the pastor, you will help people process through these life changes. And, when you know you must make adjustments in the church, you must be gentle with people. The more mature an individual is, the faster they can process change. The more immature the individual, the longer it takes.

One common mistake I made as a pastor is that when people did not enthusiastically adopt changes or decisions that I thought were healthy and necessary, I took it personally. Because I feed off of the excitement and the acceptance of others, I was greatly disappointed by the lack of support. I was offended by the resistance from people. Don't do that! Do not react the way I did. Realize that people need to process, and people will process in different ways:

> The more mature an individual is, the faster they can process change.

Resistance

Fight or Flight. Have you heard of it? Some people will stand up and resist. Does it mean they are bad people? Does it mean they are against you? Sometimes. But not always. This just may be their dominant personality. Or, they may have been conditioned this way. You need to ignore much of their initial reaction and not hold them to every word or attitude they may reveal. Give them grace. Don't react. Respond:

Proverbs 15:1 NIV
A Gentle word turns away wrath:
But a harsh word stirs up anger.

When I see someone rise up in opposition to change, I imagine a flexed arm resisting. Rather than try to overpower the flexed arm, I wait until the arm relaxes. When an arm is relaxed, you can maneuver it quite easily. When people flex, let them flex. Let them feel heard. Validate their concerns. Wait and give it time. Many times, people just need to feel like they put up a fight. Once you let them go through this exercise, they will adequately process that change is coming, and they will relax. With change, time is on your side. Time is a powerful tool that you can use. Sometimes the best thing you can do is to just wait. Patiently.

Disengage

This is the flight response. People quit. They give up. Maybe they do not leave the church, but they move away from the action. Honestly, people who disengage are more difficult to help process, in my opinion. With people who resist, they come to you. With people who disengage, you have to go to them. This takes more intentionality. This takes more of your time.

A few years back , I learned a concept of how we are wired as humans. It really helped me. Some people are early adopters. Others are late adopters. Early adopters are wired for the fresh, new idea. They love to be on the cutting edge of technology, of fashion. Early adopters are the people who are the first to go buy the new smart phone. They are first to try the new fashion design. Late adopters are the opposite. They are apprehensive to be the first. Their mentality is that what they have works, at least for them. Late adopters do not have the desire to be first. They want to be safe. For late adopters, they would rather wait until all of the bugs are fixed on the new smart phone, and make their purchase when the device goes on sale.

I have found surprisingly that I am a late adopter. I was surprised, because I see myself as an optimist. I perceive myself as high-energy, positive, high-belief, futurist. But I do not want to go first with new ideas, new designs, new technology. Maybe it is because I like a sale, but I DO NOT go stand in line to buy the newest gadget!

People who disengage may not be quitting on you. They may be waiting on you. If they are late adopters, they are just waiting for all of the bugs to be worked out. They are waiting on the sidelines until the dust settles. With late adopters, do not over-react and feel you have to go confront them. Do not be quick to engage them. Simply show them consistency in your character and in

> **People who disengage may not be quitting on you. They may be waiting on you.**

the relationship you share with them. Engage them only on their level of comfort. If they pull back, let them. Do not push them or force them. Let the process of time, and the refinement of the change solidify. You will see them re-engage. And when they do, they will stay committed and consistent.

A Changing Game

One of the most profound changes that will happen in your church is when it begins to grow. As the church grows, your leadership role must grow. As the church grows, you must grow. What you used to do as the pastor must evolve. You cannot afford to work harder than you already are. You must work smarter. That is what this book, Strategic Pastor is all about. This means that for the church to move forward, the game must change.

This concept of the game changing comes from a friend and mentor of mine, Kadi Cole. I have to give her credit for this concept, because it is so powerful. Kadi has a gift to create pictures for people to see what is and to see how to get where we need to go.

As our Stuart Campus was growing, I was trying to figure out how I needed to grow as the Campus Pastor. I wanted to maintain the progress our church had made, but I could sense that things were changing. I wanted to manage the change well so that our church family who were so dedicated would not be left behind.

Kadi said that I needed to play a different game than I was currently playing. Because I am a guy, I am sure she was trying to paint a picture in the world of sports so I would grab a hold of her concept. She told me that when the church was new and I had a small number of people, I was able to play the game of golf (metaphorically). With a relatively small number of people to care for, I could "play golf" with just about every person. In other words, I could build relationship with everyone. I could know everyone personally. I could help everyone grow spiritually and be their personal pastor. Golf is a one on one sport. Pastors can play golf with one or two people.

As the church had grown, I had moved from playing golf to playing basketball, a team sport. In the following years, I intuitively moved to being a basketball coach that empowered players on the team. Because I am a natural team builder, I had built team around me that accomplished the ministry of the church. I had moved from a golf player to a basketball coach. I mentioned this earlier in the book, that the coach does not play the game. The coach has impact from the sidelines, as he empowers the players to do the work of the church. The players are the church. The pastor is the coach.

Kadi showed me that it was again time for the game to change. She suggested that the game needed to change to football. A football team is much larger than a basketball team. A football team does not have one coach, it has many coaches. It has an Offensive Coordinator and a Defensive Coordinator. It has defensive units and offensive units. Then it has special teams. (If you are a sports fan, you are probably wanting to correct me by telling me that Basketball has multiple coaches. I know. I know. But follow the analogy, OK?)

I realized that I needed to change the game at our Campus, because I had a bigger team. And to manage a bigger team, I needed to lead through other Coaches. I needed to be one step removed from leading everything. I needed to begin to spend more time with high capacity leaders and coaches and then let them interact with the coaches. This analogy began to make sense to me, and I was ready to go charge the field and change the game.

But here was the a-ha moment that Kadi made me aware of: "Matt, you need to first tell your people that you are changing the game on them. Don't start playing football when they think they are still playing basketball."

Wow! That hit me so hard. Just as Kadi had painted a new picture for what needed to change for the church to flourish, I needed to paint that same picture for our people. If I failed to do so, I would disappoint people by moving to a new model that they did not grasp, and I would end up frustrated that people were not playing the game. When they did not understand the new game

> **People cannot embrace what they cannot grasp.**

we are now playing, the concept was still out of reach. I needed to help lead them through a necessary transition to where they could get a handle on the new structure in relationship.

I began planning a gathering of my top hundred people in the church, my Inner Circle families and leaders. I decided to call it a "huddle", to help create a theme that I would introduce. We brought footballs for people to toss around and we had a tailgate party.

It was at this huddle where I shared this new concept that we needed to change the game so that we can maintain the momentum that God was giving us. I clarified what this meant for me and for them. I had my coaches and key leaders there that I pointed to and affirmed as rising voices within our church family. I assured people that I was still their pastor, and that I loved them all dearly. I was available to them. But I explained how I would interact with them would begin to look different. I would focus on leading the church and on developing leaders. I wanted each of them to grow as leaders, and I was committed to helping anyone who was willing to pay the price to come with me. I shared the vision of where we could rise to, if we all took a step up in our growth and our capacity.

The meeting went great. People loved it. They understood. They were on board. They were excited because they saw where we were currently, and where we intended to go. After the meeting, people would call me "Coach", just to have fun with me. The leaders who I pointed to now felt affirmed, but also felt a heavier weight of responsibility than they had ever felt before. When these leaders shared their apprehension with me of their greater role, I just responded with "welcome to leadership."

In order for your church to keep moving forward with momentum, you need to embrace change. In fact, as the pastor, you need to bring change...constantly. Are you causing people pain? Yes! When you bring change, you may need to help people understand that the game is changing. The rules are changing. Paint a picture for them, and point to where you are in the picture and where they are. This will help them more quickly embrace the needed change within the church.

In this chapter, you see a common theme that is threaded through the entire book. The church is made up of people. As a Strategic Pastor, learn to identify different personalities. Study how people process life and change. When you understand how people think and engage with you, you will handle with greater care and timing.

This next chapter will be a popular chapter that many pastors will be anxious to dive in to, I am sure. Why? Because if you have lead a church for any amount of time, you have felt stuck. You have found yourself staring dead center at an obstacle, not allowing you to lead your church forward. Is it a building? A budget? A bully? Is it a mountain? A giant? A red sea? Every pastor has hit a lid keeping them from experiencing church growth and impact. I want to touch on some of the lids I have experienced and share how I learned from them. Maybe what I have been through will help you break beyond your obstacle.

Chapter 9   People Problems

Study Questions

Describe one example when you had to help a person in your church deal with a change happening within the church. Or, maybe it was a transition that you had to lead many people through. What were the pain points for you? Where did people get stuck? How did you deal with it effectively? What were mistakes you made?

What bothers you the most? People who resist? Or people who disengage? Why? What does this tell you about your personality?

When considering how the game (the church structure) will change as the church grows and matures, what sport best describes where your church is currently? How does the game you are playing need to change in order to grow?

Chapter 10

Overcoming Obstacles for Church Growth

Any pastor who has had the calling to lead a church, or even just lead a team within a church has experienced road blocks. Caring for a church family is tough enough. Leading the organization and the people to growth and impact is another challenge altogether.

Don't you hate road blocks? Especially when you are on your way to an appointment. I do not like to waste time. I like to leave for an appointment at the last possible moment so that I arrive right on time. Not early, not late. Exactly on time. My wife challenges me that I do not allow enough extra time for my trip. She reminds me that traffic may be tight. Weather may slow me down. Or, I may run in to road blocks. I usually disregard her warnings, but, as it turns out, she is usually right. Well...honestly, she is always right. I don't allow enough time to travel to where I need to be. As a result, I cause a lot of unnecessary stress for myself when I travel.

I have navigational issues. Meaning, I can't navigate. My closest friends know this too well. When guys travel with me in my car, I will be telling a dramatic story, and they will interrupt me to remind me to make the right turn. God blessed my life when He created Google maps. Well, Google created this app, but who gave them the inspiration??

I love Google Maps because I can simply follow the quickest path to where I am going. The problem is when the map takes me to a street that has a road block. Ugh! Florida is a great state, and they are always improving the roads. I love this progress, but not when I am trying to get somewhere. Not when I have allowed just enough time to show up before my event starts. I know, I need to work on this. Pray for me.

I think pastors feel this kind of stress when they are trying to lead their church to growth and impact. They have navigated the clearest path that gets them there in the quickest way possible. But, as fate would have it, or maybe Satan himself, there is an unforeseen road block.

Detour, 5 miles south.

Road closed.

Turn around, go back the way you came and go South another 10 miles.

When people are depending on you to lead them, but you are confronted with a road block, you experience frustration. Can I hear an amen?

I want to discuss some of the obstacles you will likely face as you attempt to lead your church to the next level of growth and impact. And, like my wife warns me before I leave for an appointment, these road blocks should not be a surprise to you. You should beware of them. You should expect them along the way. And, you can learn how to navigate them strategically.

Finances

This is an obvious one. You find out quickly when you want to put your vision in to action that you need money, and lots of it. I know God can do anything, and I know He has all of the resources. I know that faith can move mountains. But your faith to do what God wants to do through you and your church requires finances. Most of us are not good at dealing with finances. I mean, you did not go to Seminary to study for ministry because you were a fundraiser, or an accountant. You were called to preach and to be a pastor.

When we think about having to talk about money to our church family, most of us shutter. We visualize a televangelist selling holy water and trinkets on tv to beg people to give. We do not want to be labeled a prosperity preacher. And yet, to fund the vision, we need provision. Asking people for money to fund the church is not a natural skill for us. But at some point, we will need to learn how to do this. Otherwise, finances will always be an obstacle for our church growing and reaching to the level that God intends.

Before joining Christ Fellowship, I started a church with a couple of friends who shared a common dream with me. It was exciting. We had some families that were enthusiastic to start with us and so we all met in a borrowed office space for our first planning meeting. My friend, Nate Carter was going to be the Lead Pastor, and Chris McKnown and I were there to support him as pastors. Nate asked the group to give sacrificially at the meeting, and we raised enough money to rent a local school auditorium for the first couple of months. We soon started the church with a great showing of people. I led the music and Chris led the students. We all took on additional duties to ensure that all bases were covered.

As we looked ahead toward the Christmas season, I wanted to produce a Christmas service with a special musical production that our church family could invite the community to. Christmas was a prime opportunity to show the community our new church launch. But we barely had enough money to rent the school for Sunday mornings and had just a few small resources to get by. There was no money for anything extra.

I asked Nate if I could raise the needed money for rent of the school and resources to pull off a Christmas production. He gave me his blessing, but I am sure he doubted that I would have any success. People were already giving sacrificially so we could start our new church. Yet, I believed so much in this opportunity to build our church, that I committed that I would somehow raise the money. We had started the church with about 100 people. My prayer goal was to triple that for our Christmas service. Ambitious. Crazy.

I began calling people in the church who I knew had the financial means to help. I thought of people I had built relationship with, even if in a small way. I shared the vision of what I wanted to do for our church, and then asked boldly "I need three people to give a thousand dollars to cover our expenses. I am asking you if will be one of those three." I got some who declined. I got some who said they would think about it. But I got three wo said "I can do that, Pastor Matt."

When I got an affirmative answer, I became even more bold and said "let me come meet you at your office now and grab a check from you. I need to rent the school auditorium this week." They were a bit taken back, but all three people agreed. I drove to their business, received the check and thanked them for making this Christmas community outreach possible for our new church. I had never asked for money before. I could not believe I had actually pushed myself to ask people. And, I could not believe that people actually responded to me.

Do you know that our one hundred faithful people brought friends and family with them and we had over three hundred and fifty people attend that Christmas production? Nate, the pastor was shocked that I retrieved the money. Our church had pulled off an awesome first Christmas production having triple the Sunday attendance come!

That experience broadened my faith in God. It emboldened me to ask people to serve and to give. I was not able to pay musicians or audio engineers. I had to ask professionals I knew to give their talent freely. It was scary to

> **Leadership requires asking others to give big and serve big.**

ask people to give. It was discouraging to hear some "no"s, especially from friends I thought would step up when I asked. But leadership requires asking others to give big and serve big .

Sell the Vision

I have learned the art of asking people to give their money for the mission of the church. I have developed the skill of asking people to give their time to serve in the church. When I was in my college years, I worked at Macys Department store in the summer breaks. I was working to save money, but ended up spending most of my earned money on food, games and clothes. I worked in the Men's clothing department selling clothes to customers. The department manager set quota selling goals for each sales representative. We were measured by our volume of sales. I hated the sales quotas, because I hated the idea of selling.
Actually, I was quite good at selling and made sale associate of the month twice. One month I received a 25 cent raise – whoopee! I hated selling because I felt that I was manipulating customers. I wondered if they thought I was being nice to them simply to get them to buy more merchandise. I would complement them, but wondered if they thought I was truly being genuine. I remember telling one of my co-workers "I will never work in sales. I am going to be a pastor of a great church."

Little did I know that there is some "selling" involved in being a pastor. Oh yes, to get the church moving forward to growth and impact, you must "sell" people on the vision of the church. If you think people just freely part with their money, think again. People do not come up to you offering to park cars in the church parking lot. People do not get excited about changing diapers of crying babies in the church nursery. You will find that it is not natural for people to give or to serve.

Most people come to church with a consumer mindset. They are looking for care, for healing, and for relationship. Single people are looking for a spouse. Parents are looking for someone to fix their teenagers. People are primarily thinking of themselves. They are focused on their needs. They do not naturally see the mission of the church like you do. As the pastor, you must become skilled at learning to "sell" the vision to the people in a compelling and inspiring way that will capture their hearts and activate their minds.

As I said before, I hate the idea of selling. It feels cheap and misleading. I do not want to be selling anything to anyone in the church. My heart is to help people by leading them to Jesus Christ. My desire is to build God's church. What has helped me get more comfortable with asking people to serve and give is that I believe with all my heart that what I am asking people to give to is worthy of their investment. You see, I am bought in to what I am called to do. I am sold out to Jesus, both me and my family. I am a product of the church. I am healthy and developed because of the church.

We must remember that the church is God's idea. Jesus started the church. He died for the church. My family and I willingly and joyfully serve in the church, give our money to God through the ministry of the church. So, when I stand up on Sunday morning and offering plates are being passed, I do not apologize for asking people to give sacrificially, and to give systematically as the Bible instructs.

There is a skill to asking people to give and to serve. Part of that skill is to know when to push and when to back off. If one Sunday I have given a teaching on tithing and then call people to sacrificially give, I will follow up the next week by thanking our church for their heart of generosity and faithfulness. Another way I can communicate the principle of giving and serving is by having others in the church share their story of giving.

When you share a great vision to grow and expand, you will need to ask people to give in a greater way than they think they can. Be ready for mean letters and snide comments. As the pastor, you must not let these comments discourage you. When people struggle with your challenge to give, it may mean that they are struggling in their own issues of control. While you can receive constructive comments from good people, do not let people who are not commited to the mission of the church intimidate you.

Do not get distracted. Your critics are not called by God to steward the vision that He gave you. They do not know what it takes to lead people. If they did, they would not oppose you, but would instead rally around you.

When you are challenging people to trust God and to invest in His holy church, you are literally being the voice of God to the people. You are giving them an opportunity to respond to God, not to you. You are the messenger. God is the leader. Let God deal with people. You obey God, pastor.

Facility

Facility can be an obstacle to further growth. You may be at the stage where you need to find a larger meeting space. You may not even have a permanent facility at this stage of your church. Like me years ago, you may be having portable church in a borrowed space. Some of you may even have your church meeting in homes. What you are doing now is working. But to reach more people, you will have to address the limitations of your facilities. Of course, facilities have a direct correlation to your church's finances, which is why I started with that subject first.

Taking a step forward to bigger and better facilities is truly a huge step. It changes everything. It means possibly changing location in town. It means possibly taking on debt. It means remodel. It means that you as the pastor will be forced to ascribe much of your time to managing building projects and finances. But if you do not address the need for more facility when your church is ready to grow, you will stifle growth.

Create Space

I believe that when you create space, the natural reaction is that the space fills up. I call this the vacuum principle. Space is consumed. Can I prove this? Yes. In my garage at home.

Shortly after we bought our home in Stuart, I decided to create more space in our home for me to have some of my studio equipment and man-cave stuff. We have a 3 bedroom home and I wanted my own space. So, I got creative and enclosed part of our garage with drywall to create my own room. I painted it and put a portable A/C unit in the wall. It was great! I had my music equipment set up and a small living room set up with a tv and movie center. I made it clear to Kellie, my wife that this room was mine and that it was off limits to her. She had reign over the entire house. My kingdom was clearly marked in the garage. She agreed… in theory.

Slowly, Kellie's spa equipment ended up in there. As our kids grew, Kellie wanted to keep their toys and baby clothes. Then, Kellie decided we needed a treadmill so she could exercise. (I can't remember one time she used that treadmill.) Before long, the room was filled with stuff. What happened to my tidy, spacious "extra room?" The vacuum effect.

Most of us have heard the famous line from the classic movie, Field of Dreams "if you build it, they will come." That may be true, but we know as pastor, growth does not just happen. But, I do believe creating space allows for growth. Sure, you can add more services on the weekends. You can makeshift a student ministry space together. You can buy some more cupboards to store children's toys in. But, creating more space is a must in order for your church to go to the next level.

How much more space do you need? How big is too big? What if your church cannot afford the cost? All good questions. Every situation is different. Every church is in a position of what they can afford and what they can handle. But, to answer the question, I would say bigger. More. And I would say bigger than you first would guess. You need more classrooms for children. You need a bigger foyer. You need a larger platform. You need twice the parking lot. You need more office space. You need more storage space. You need a bigger auditorium, a lot bigger.

You may not have many staff right now. But as God blesses, you will add staff. Maybe your staff will be more great volunteers, but they will need space to work. You may not have many children yet in your children ministry. But you are going to get better at attracting more young families. If you don't have multiple rooms open, you will not keep those young families. You may see storage space as wasted space. But you will soon begin to be more creative with ministries and services, and will need a place to stage those pieces. That space will allow you do provide some great resources for group ministry, student ministry, young adult ministry. Your music and media team will love you for having more storage space.

> Give your church room to grow in to.

Acquiring more facility means that your church will have to stretch financially. It will take an act of faith to step out beyond what you can afford now, what you need now. Yet, when you create more space for your church, you will watch God fill it. Of course, you have to lead the growth. You have to make sure the church is headed in the right direction, and doing the healthy things I have been talking about in this book. But my point here is that if you do not think bigger and broader, even the most healthy church will stay small. A plant must be put in a bigger pot of soil for it to growth bigger and taller. If you keep the plant in a small pot, the plant will stay small. Think bold and big. Stretch your faith and broaden your plan for a bigger facility.

Function

In order to allow for more church growth and greater impact, you need to consider how your church functions. How does your church staff function? What does your church Elder Board expect of you as the pastor? If you are on staff as one of the Associate Pastors, what does your Senior Pastor expect of you? What you may be doing now may be working well within the church. The way the church staff function together now is good. But what you are doing now will not be good enough for when the church is bigger, when the church is doing more ministry.

John Maxwell says "what got you here won't take you there." This is such a great challenge to us. This does not mean what you are doing now is bad. In fact, it is good. It led your church to the place of health and impact that you see today. Yet, in order to prepare for the next level, you must first change your function. You must change the way your team functions.

When I discussed getting a bigger facility earlier, I challenged you to create space. With regard to the way the church teams function, the same is true. When you think of your work load and your responsibilities, you need to create some space. I am talking about making margin in your ministry. To do this, you must STOP DOING some of what you are doing now. You need to ask yourself what leadership you can begin handing over to other worthy leaders. I like to challenge myself to hand over 25% of my responsibility and ministry to others around me so I have that 25% extra margin to begin doing higher-leverage work. Do the same for yourself. Then challenge those who you give more to hand over 25% of what they currently do to trusted people in their lives.

Discuss this shift in function with your staff team. Share this shift with your Elder Board. Communicate well with your volunteers and key families. Prepare your people for a shift in how the team functions and how the church must function to position you for greater growth and impact.

I recently shifted the function of our Stuart Campus staff and leaders so we were prepared for the growth and impact God wants to bring to our church. I sensed that God wanted to take us to another level. I see with spiritual eyes the opportunity to initiate, to invest and to impact. We have open doors in the schools, in the Sheriff's Office, and in the community. There are great people within our church family who are leaning in and are ready for more. There are faithful followers who are ready to become a leader. There are young people I see with a calling on their life for ministry. There are churches and pastors who are wanting mentoring and wanting support to grow.

I began sharing this vision with my Senior Pastor and my boss. I then shared this with my Inner Circle leaders. I then brought this vision to my staff and some key families. I spread the vision like seed cast in to the soil. The next step was not to start working on the vision. It was to prepare myself and prepare my team by changing the function of the team. I needed to create space in how we function, in order to accomplish this greater vision. That meant I had to give up some leadership that I was doing.

I gave funerals and pastor care to one pastor. To do this, I spent time showing him and teaching him. To another pastor, I handed over baptisms and community serve projects. I spent time connecting him with my key leaders and strategic partners within the community. I began investing in some of my key families through other pastors. This was difficult for me, because I want to be close to our key families. But in order to create margin in my ministry, I had to begin leading one step removed. I am a relational person. I am energized by people and long or relationship. I sense when people need more attention, more care. And yet, I had to resist this tendency to respond. I had to begin to care and connect through others.

The team around me gladly stepped in to these new roles. However, I warned them that their current roles could not suffer. They were still responsible for their current role AND the additional leadership I was putting on them. I began holding them accountable to who they were going to empower. I challenged them to find key leaders that they could bring around them to help carry the weight. This is the Inner Circle I mentioned earlier. I gave them the challenge: Who are your 12? Who are your 3? Where did I come up with that? Watching Jesus. The Inner Circle principle is to define some great people and bring them around you for this season. Once your Inner Circle has a grasp of what they are to lead, you begin enjoying some margin.

Who are your 12? Who are your 3? Pastor, YOU are the lid to your church growing. You are the obstacle to seeing your church have more impact. Sorry to put pressure on you. You are the leader. You need to evaluate your current function and figure out how to expand your it. Try taking away just 25% of what you do currently. Give it away. Create space to remove the function obstacle.

In this last chapter, we will discuss the nuances of the life of being a pastor. To be a pastor requires more than fulfilling a job description. It is a calling. There is a defined lifestyle. In order to remain effective and healthy for many years, we must adhere to healthy habits and right thinking. These recommendations will help us stay in a zone where God can work in us and through us to do His holy work of pastor.

Chapter 10   Overcoming Obstacles to Growth Your Church

Study Questions

Describe a financial obstacle that you have faced. What brought you the most fear? What skills do you think you needed in order to lead your church past the obstacle?

What obstacles do you see now with your facility? Why are they limiting your growth and impact? What is your dream facility? Begin to form a vision with your team of a greater facility or space and think through when the right time to campaign for this greater vision for more space and resources.

How does your team function? Specifically, what are your primary roles as pastor? How can you re-structure your staff and leaders to function at a higher level so that you free up space for you? List your current 5 main functions. Be mindful: do not list what you hope to be, or what you should be. Rather, list what you spend a majority of your time doing now.

Your Current Main Functions:

_____

_____

_____

_____

_____

Chapter 11

A Pastor's Life

The essence of being a pastor is that you are giving to people. More than leading people or growing a church, you are giving yourself to others. We are modeling our life after Jesus Christ. One scripture that I keep close in my view is found in Matthew 20:28 when Jesus said:

I have not come to be served, but to serve and to give my life as a ransom for many.

When you sign up to be a pastor, you begin to understand this verse. Do not ever regret this life, if God has called you to it. It is the most thrilling, most significant calling you could give yourself to. God will reward you in Heaven one day. But the great news is, He will reward you every day on Earth. To be used of God is miraculous. To see God working in us to fulfill a holy purpose is the most beautiful use of our time and gifts.

I believe that those who work closely with God walk closely with God. We see this with the Bible heroes we studied in the first chapter. Moses was invited in to the Tabernacle of Meeting to talk with God as one friend talks with another. Samuel heard God speak directly to Him. David received plans to build God's temple. Paul encountered Jesus face to face, and was inspired by

> # Those who work closely with God walk closely with God.

the Holy Spirit to write letters which would become Holy Scripture. Jesus heard His Father's voice say "This is My Son in Whom I am well pleased."

As a pastor, you will hear God and you will see God in a beautiful way as you follow Him closely. Please do not think that all of my strategies and skills replace the need to hear from God! On the contrary, we are NOTHING without God. He truly is the Leader. You are the follower. The Apostle Paul made this clear when He stated:

I Corinthians 11:1
Follow me as I follow Christ.

As God's pastor to His people, you need to keep an appropriate posture. Keep yourself humble and usable before God, and be sure to live with these principles in mind:

A Life of Sacrifice

When we start out as a pastor, sacrificing is not as difficult to manage. Most pastors I know have to sacrifice quite a bit in the beginning. Many pastors come from successful careers. They had built up possessions and a nice lifestyle through hard work and achievement in the business world. When God calls them to ministry, there is usually a reduction in salary, or sometimes, no salary. Whether they are starting a new church, or stepping in to a church, most pastors start small. I know some pastors who literally use their own money to pay the rent on the church property. They actually cover some of their own expenses for the small, struggling church they are caring for. It takes time to build up a church family who learn the Biblical principle of tithing and investing in their church before a pastor can draw a livable salary and then afford other staff and resources.

In this season of my ministry, I have now been blessed with more hired staff, with a permanent facility to have church, and with a bigger budget to do ministries. The temptation sometimes is to go in to cruise control and ease off. But I know that to ask others to sacrifice means I must always lead the way. I understand clearly that I must always practice what I preach – well, actually, practice what Jesus preached. I am always looking for ways I can sacrifice in my life to keep me humble and hungry for God, so He will continue to use my life.

The lifestyle of sacrifice is so beautiful, and so necessary. When we sacrifice, it means we are giving up something that is precious to us. It can be money, but it can also be a possession. Sometimes, the sacrifice comes when we have to give an unfair amount of time and energy. This can be the greatest sacrifice we may give, because a pastor is already giving a lot to the church. When we truly sacrifice, it does something deep within our soul. Sacrifice helps us feel and relate to what Jesus felt. There is a giving up, a giving over of ourselves that is a spiritual moment in our lives. We cannot ask our people to give up and sacrifice if we are not sacrificing.

When the pastor sacrifices first, the people will follow. Sacrifice inspires like nothing else. Sacrifice reveals our heart. For me, sacrifice breaks my heart. It deals with my selfishness and self-centeredness. I am able to fully release my choke hold on my money, my possessions and my control to God. There is a beautiful breaking that happens deep inside of me. And because I am the spiritual model for our church family, I become a catalyst for others to experience the same spiritual breakthrough for others.

> When the pastor sacrifices first, the people will follow.

Sacrifice is worship to God

When we sacrifice something of value, we are making a profound statement before God. We are proclaiming that He is above all things in our life. He is first. We are demonstrating our love and our worship to God. When done with a pure motive to love God and to serve people, God receives our worship as a sweet aroma. He is pleased with our act of sacrifice.

Sacrifice is trust in God

By sacrificing something of value which we possess, we are declaring that God will make up the difference. God will supply our needs. We are making a statement of faith that God is more than enough. I love this. We can put the pressure on God to come through for us. I believe God loves to take care of us, especially when we become dependent on Him. As the pastor, we get to teach our people in real time how to trust God. This is a great object lesson for the people who are looking to us to model a life of trust in God. We are drawing them away from the world's system of holding on to what we have and acquiring more possessions. Rather, we are pulling them towards the Kingdom of God, which says we are to give freely and serve others, knowing that God is the source of every good thing. God has an unlimited supply and He will take care of us!

A Life of Sacredness

A pastor is to be an example to others in how to live. We should strive to look like Jesus. We need to treat the calling on our lives as sacred and holy. Holy means to be set apart for a specific purpose. There are times when I would like to be judged just like a normal person. There are moments when I wonder what it would feel like to just let loose and do what I want and say what I think. However, I am keenly aware that to have God's anointing on my life is a privilege. It is sacred. I remember that I must treat the calling of pastor with great care and reverence.

In the Bible, there is a story that shows a man who was carrying the Ark of the Covenant for King David. The Ark was in danger of falling and the man reached out to grab it. God had instructed no one to touch the Ark, and when the man touched the Ark, he died. (1 Samuel 6:7) This is a sobering reminder that God's presence and God's calling are sacred to Him and we should remember to handle our position and our assignment with care.

Practically, we remain sacred before God and before men by what we practice and by what we refrain from. A holy life is lived out well by what we celebrate and by what we do not tolerate. When you accept the high calling of pastor, you are declaring that you are a man of God. You are holy, set apart for His special use, His holy purpose. You are also setting yourself up as an example of how to follow God and honor Him. This is a serious step you are taking that requires some big decisions for your lifestyle.
For everyone, this will look different. Based on your own convictions, you must choose what holy living looks like for you. For me, I have made some conscious choices of what I will do and what I will not do. I am not perfect. I admit I can be inconsistent. I have struggles and weaknesses like everyone else. But I do remain true to what I strive to be and what decisions I work to uphold in my personal life.

Public Life vs. Personal Life

For the pastor, there can be no separation between our public life and our personal life. We all have seen too many public figures think that they can hide some of their personal life from the public. But we only have one life. And what we are eventually spills over in to the public, whether we want it to or not. This is why the calling of pastor must come from the inside of our life. It must be the heart and soul of our being. One cannot be pastor for fifty hours a week, and then be something different when we are home. While we need healthy separation from work and pressure, we never leave our calling in God. This is why having the reminder of our sacred calling must always be at the forefront of our thinking.

Possessions and Ownership

In my conviction, I believe that our sacred calling requires that we give up a sense of ownership. To be called of God to be his man requires a giving up of one's self. Everything we own is God's anyway. But I believe that we need to not see our possessions as our own, but as God's. He allows us to use them and enjoy them. But we belong to God as set apart, and we do not own anything. As a pastor, I believe God supernaturally takes care of us and our personal needs. We see with the Jewish priests how God did not want them to be owners, as God wanted to personally provide for them. God was their portion:

Deuteronomy 18:1-2 NIV
The Levitical priests—indeed, the whole tribe of Levi—are to have no allotment or inheritance with Israel. They shall live on the food offerings presented to the Lord, for that is their inheritance. 2 They shall have no inheritance among their fellow Israelites; the Lord is their inheritance, as he promised them.

Now, I am certainly not saying we cannot be land owners. I am not saying we cannot purchase a home or a car. I own a home and own cars. We do not have to live a life of poverty. live a life of poverty. What I am trying to communicate is a mindset of not being concerned with building up possessions for ownership. Rather, your focus is your calling, not your career. Your mindset is that God will take care of your needs, so that you can give yourself fully to His purposes. To practice this in my own life, sometimes I will kneel in the middle of my house and declare to God "this is all yours, God. I dedicate all of this to you. It's not mine. Use y life for your holy purpose."

> # A life of Sacredness says that you belong to God.

A life of Sacredness says that you belong to God. Your gifts, your possessions are not yours. They are to be given freely to God for His calling. When we put our lives in His hand, He blesses us and makes us holy.

A Life of Significance

Some aspects of being a pastor can feel mundane. There have been times when I wondered if I was making any difference. When you are investing in people, You wonder if you will ever see fruit come from them. When you are always helping wounded people, you wonder if you will ever see them heal and grow strong.

What I would encourage you to remember is that the longer you work as a pastor, the more impact you will see. I have been a pastor for 25 years. I am starting to see more great stories of impact in people than ever before. Part of why I felt led to write this book is because I realize just how much God has used my life. Today, I have an overwhelming sense of significance, not because I am great, but because God is great.

The Bible teaches the principle of sowing and reaping:

Galatians 6:7-10
Do not be deceived: God cannot be mocked. A man reaps what he sows. Whoever sows to please their flesh, from the flesh will reap destruction; whoever sows to please the Spirit, from the Spirit will reap eternal life. Let us not become weary in doing good, for at the proper time we will reap a harvest if we do not give up. Therefore, as we have opportunity, let us do good to all people, especially to those who belong to the family of believers.

This passage is not simply a "give and you will receive" teaching. It is embedded in a passage of scripture that is teaching how we invest our lives in believers. It is encouraging us that as we care for people and help them grow healthy, we will see a great harvest in their lives. As you stay faithful and stay invested, you will see that your life truly has great significance through others. Don't give up! Don't quit doing what you are doing. You may be in a seed planting season, so don't expect to see crops just yet. Wait on the process. You will one day look and realize that you have had significance!

What the Doctor Ordered

To sustain the rigorous regimen a pastor will endure through years of ministry, you must learn to make health a priority. You need to tend to your health physically, emotionally, relationally, and mentally. Remember my statement I mentioned earlier in this book: "God, You are God. I am not."

You are a human being, just like all of the people you look after. You have a body, you have emotions, you have limitations. You have to pay the bills, plan for dinner for your family, and manage stress levels like everybody else. Just like a physician should take the advice he gives to his patients, you should practice your own teaching.

I want to challenge you in some specific areas, although there are many facets of health we could discuss. Allow me to be your pastor for a minute. Listen to the "doctor" as I prescribe some good medicine so you can remain healthy:

Sabbath

Do you take it? Sunday is your Sabbath, you say? I beg to differ.

I argue that Sunday is not a true Sabbath for the pastor. You and your family are providing a Sabbath experience for people, but it is not for you and your family. Sunday is game day. You are focused, giving out, working hard. You need to set aside a day a week for rest, worship, reflection, fun. This day cannot be your catch-up day, where you are doing all of your personal chores or helping family or neighbors. You need to fill up and replenish.

This day will look different for you than for other pastors. For me, I find it hard to truly detach from the responsibilities of a fast-paced Multi-Site Church structure. Because I live out my principle of loving people when they need me, I cannot completely isolate myself for twenty-four hours. What I have been doing that seems to work for me is to split my Sabbath between Mondays and Fridays. I am able to detach about 90% on both days, thereby allowing me the needed time to replenish back to 100%.

I have found that the more responsibility I take on as a pastor and in my personal life, the more time I need alone. I need more time in solitude, quiet, still, hidden. I have learned this only in the last couple of years. My natural tendency is to be always going, always with people. I find that I am much like a smart phone. Because I am expending more energy often, I need to recharge often. When I work, I am intense. I need to balance my intensity with calm, easy, simple. Because you are a delicate, complex being, you cannot run at high intensity all of the time. You will wear out fast. You need to create more balance in your life. You need slow. I remember Pastor Rich Guerra coached me once by teaching me this principle "I don't let my highs get too high, and I don't let my lows get too low." That is great leadership of self.

Experiment with your week and block off your life a few times a week for yourself and your family and friends.

Mentor

This is more difficult than it sounds. I know. Why is it so hard for pastors to find mentors? I think it is challenging because we have a hard time asking for help. We know what it feels like to always be leaned upon by people to mentor them, so we would never want to do that to another pastor. Because we are pastors, we suppose that there is nothing that another pastor is going to do or say that will help us. We already know what he is going to say. How will that help me?

> A Pastor needs a Pastor more than any other person.

Listen to me: a pastor needs a pastor more than any other person. Do you know why? Because a pastor can feel as alone as anyone else. In some ways, a pastor can feel more alone. That is because so few people know what it is like to be the leader, to be the person carrying the weight.

A pastor carrying the weight of leadership without oversight is a dangerous thing.

I actively seek out mentors and pastors to hold me accountable and speak in to my life. I also seek out pastors who are my peers that I can find friendship and support in. These people have kept me grounded when I was off balance and have created accountability that help me stay on course. Inviting a mentor and a pastor in your life is essential. Meet with them regularly. Just like you get your car's oil changed every 3000 miles, get your tune up with your mentor regularly. God will not trust someone who is not accountable to others.

Gears

As a pastor, you will journey through different seasons in your ministry. Your twenties will look different than your thirties. Your forties will look different than your fifties. Just like you understand that you can work out in the gym as intense when you are older, the same is true as a pastor.

I think it is wise to understand how to move in to different gears as you move in to different seasons. You need to learn to shift gears based on your season of life. What you tried to lead in your thirties, you likely need to lead in a different way. How you lead when you just start in a new position would be very different if you have now been in the same position a while. Let me explain.

When I first launched our Stuart Campus, I knew that there would be a lot of physical labor involved. While I do not naturally like physical labor, I understood that I needed to lead the charge so that people would join in to set up the church every week. I knew that investing sweat equity was the right thing to do in order to win over people's respect. This was a season of hard plowing and planting seeds.

In the beginning years, I felt it was important to personally visit every home group that was meeting around the County, thirty-five total. I made those rounds the first three years. I actually enjoyed that part, but gained weight when I was invited to enjoy all of the food.

In this season of my leadership, I do not have the same margin in my schedule to visit every home group. I do not have the same energy level to do all of the manual labor, all of the set up and tear down as I did when I was younger. But because I have built teams and developed leaders who know me and respect me, I am able to lean on them to put in their sweat equity.

I have learned not to allow myself to feel guilty about this, or try to explain to others my season. I know in my heart that I have paid that price and that God has me leading other things now. Don't get me wrong. I always find a place to carry equipment, serve people and even visit some groups. But I am now focused on calling up young, passionate leaders who remind me of when I started. I give them the opportunity to respond to God's call in their lives. I can be a foundation of credibility and experience that they can stand on to begin leading the church.

Who You Are

The last thought I want to give you is this:

It's not what you do, it's who you are

This principal has helped me get re-focused on the essence of my calling as pastor. I can get so worried about what I am doing for God, that I forget about who I am becoming for God.

Pastor, your life speaks louder than your actions. Live in such a way that people see Jesus. It is your faithfulness. It is your love for God. It is your relationship with God.

A great scripture passage that Jesus taught is found in the book of Mark:

Mark 8:36 (paraphrased)
What good is it if a man gains the whole world, but loses his own soul?

In relating to a pastor and his ministry, I would like to change the focus of this verse, in order to apply it directly to us:

What good is it if a pastor wins the world for Jesus, but does not truly know Jesus himself?

Over the years, I have written out personal mission statements. I have practiced the discipline of writing out objectives, so that I have a clear focus of what I am striving for. One thing that I practice when I do this is to try to picture an image of what I want to be. I have always looked to great people who are examples. I have been inspired by different people who had a quality that I wanted to attain in my own life.

In my teens, I looked to great musicians as models to follow. In my later years, I aspired to be a great pastor, so it was successful pastors who I studied. More recently, I have been intrigued by leadership. My attention is drawn to those who have led courageously and strategically.

When it comes to the very essence of who I aspire to be, I think of one particular man found in the Bible. I am drawn to this man not because of his gifts or accomplishments. I am not focused on this man because of his particular personality or character trait. I am focused on him for one key factor the the Bible mentions about him. The man I am focusing on Enoch.

The Bible does does not give great detail of Enoch. While I have mentioned many great heroes in the Bible, like, Moses, David, Jesus, Enoch is described as simply "a man who walked with God."

Genesis 5:24 NIV
Enoch walked faithfully with God; then he was no more, because God took him away.

For me, to have it be said that I walked with God would be the greatest achievement I could ever hope for. While I want to achieve great things for God, I want it said of me that I walked faithfully with Him.

As a pastor, we must first and foremost walk with God. Walking with Him requires close proximity to Him. It speaks of intimacy and openness. To walk with Him means we are following close behind Him. We are attentive. We are listening and watching.

In this book, I have shared strategies and mindset that help you see great impact in your ministry as a Strategic Pastor. They all have to do with growing as a leader. When you grow in your leadership skills, more people will follow you. However, the greatest leadership skill I could give you is this:

When you walk with God, you will catch His presence

When you catch His presence, others will want to walk with you

God's presence brings with it God's power and anointing. This is the most attractional, most compelling component you can attain to get people to follow you. And yet, none of us would DARE try to attain this for the purpose of use! God forbid! Rather, we long for God's presence for our very existence, for our pleasure and blessing. The true joy is not what we accomplish. It is to know God and to walk closely with Him. The outflow of this blessing is that we simply bring others along with us on the journey.

Conclusion

Church ministry is all – encompassing. When a pastor begins to look at all of the needs of the church, and tries to care for every person in the church, he becomes overwhelmed very quickly. With little resources and many

obstacles, we are seeing many pastors giving up. Pastors today are lonely, wounded, tired, and stuck.

However, our country needs vibrant, relevant churches now more than ever. With other religions like Islam on the rise, and with a post Christian culture of humanism and even Satanism growing in America, people are looking for truth and hope. The Church is the answer to the cry of the world! The Church is where restoration of marriage and family takes place. The Church is where Biblical truth is taught, which is the foundation of the rule of law and absolutes are proven. The Church is where care for the poor and the orphan comes from. The Church is where the arts flourish and people's gifts are developed.

The Church is the greatest endeavor we could ever give ourselves to. No business, no talent, no amount of money could be as worthy of our life than the mission of the Church. Jesus, the very Son of God started the Church. HIS heart and mission was the Church. Jesus was the Strategic Pastor that we should look to in HOW to build His Church.

Jesus built His Church on people. He invested in twelve willing men. These men invested in people. Through the centuries, pastors and missionaries have carried on the assignment Jesus gave them:

Ephesians 2:20-22 NLT
This family is built on the teachings of the missionaries and the early preachers. Jesus Christ Himself is the cornerstone, which is the most important part of the building. Christ keeps this building together and it is growing into a holy building for the Lord. You are also being put together as a part of this building because God lives in you by His Spirit.

When you see the legacy of leaders down through the ages, when you consider the Apostles, and even the Bible heroes like Moses, Samuel and David, you begin to realize the significance of the time we are living in. We are living in the End Times. We are the pastors and missionaries that Jesus has called for today. He is depending on us to build His House, His Church. The Church is more relevant now than it has ever been. The Church is more powerful than it has ever been!

Now is the time to begin to build up, pray up and speak up. Get a bigger vision for your church, pastor. Get a stronger passion. Get an inner circle of people around you – people who share your heart, your enthusiasm, and your grit. Get some TOUGH PEOPLE. No wimps. Pastor Tommy Barnett told a group of pastors "I only spend time with people who share my vision." I love that! I love everyone unconditionally. But I invest myself strategically.

Pray hard, but work strategically

Love well, but invest strategically

Dream big, but plan strategically

Chapter 11   A Pastor's Life

Study Questions

As Enoch walked with God, describe your walk with God in this season. Is this the closest you have been to God? Or, were there other times that you were closer to Him?

What is an example of sacrifice in your life, in order for you to follow God in your calling?

How are you moving away from doing to being? How does Sabbath play in to that?

Do you have a mentor? If not, what is the obstacle keeping you from finding one and meeting with them?

Thank you for reading this book. If you enjoyed this book, I would greatly appreciate if you would take the time to give a review on:

Amazon

Book Baby

http://matthewpilot.blogspot.com

https://www.facebook.com/matthewpilot

https://www.instagram.com/mattpilotstuartfl/

CPSIA information can be obtained
at www.ICGtesting.com
Printed in the USA
LVHW080548020119
602426LV00021B/1448/P

9 781513 642680